The Form and Function
of the Body of the Greek Letter

SOCIETY OF BIBLICAL LITERATURE

DISSERTATION SERIES

EDITED BY

HOWARD C. KEE

AND

DOUGLAS A. KNIGHT

Number 2

THE FORM AND FUNCTION OF THE BODY OF THE GREEK LETTER:

A STUDY OF THE LETTER-BODY

IN THE NON-LITERARY PAPYRI AND IN PAUL THE APOSTLE

by

JOHN LEE WHITE

SCHOLARS PRESS
Missoula, Montana

THE FORM AND FUNCTION OF THE BODY OF THE GREEK LETTER:

A STUDY OF THE LETTER-BODY

IN THE NON-LITERARY PAPYRI AND IN PAUL THE APOSTLE

SECOND EDITION, CORRECTED

by

JOHN LEE WHITE

PUBLISHED BY

SCHOLARS PRESS

FOR

The Society of Biblical Literature

DISTRIBUTED BY

SCHOLARS PRESS
University of Montana
Missoula, Montana 59801

THE FORM AND FUNCTION OF THE BODY OF THE GREEK LETTER:

A STUDY OF THE LETTER-BODY

IN THE NON-LITERARY PAPYRI AND IN PAUL THE APOSTLE

BY

JOHN LEE WHITE
518 South William
Columbia, Missouri 65201

Ph.D., 1970   Advisor:
Vanderbilt University   Robert W. Funk

Library of Congress Cataloging in Publication Data

White, John Lee.
    The form and function of the body of the Greek
letter.

    (Dissertation series - Society of Biblical Liter-
ature ; no. 2)
    Originally presented as the author's thesis, Van-
derbilt University, 1970.
    Bibliography: p.
    1.   Bible.   N.T.   Epistles of Paul — Criticism,
interpretation, etc.   2.   Greek letters — History and
criticism.   I.   Title.   II.   Series: Society of
Biblical Literature. Dissertation series ; no. 2.
BS2650.2.W43   1975   227'.8'06   75-33088
ISBN 0-89130-048-1

PRINTED IN THE UNITED STATES OF AMERICA
2 3 4 5
Edwards Brothers, Inc.
Ann Arbor, Michigan 48104

TABLE OF CONTENTS

LIST OF TABLES

ACKNOWLEDGMENTS

I wish to express thanks to Robert W. Funk. It was under his tutelage that I gained an appreciation, and developed the skills, of this kind of investigation.

Thanks are extended to Leander E. Keck, from whom I also learned skills necessary for the investigation and presentation of data.

I am indebted to the faculty and staff, and especially to the President-Dean, Robert K. Ordway, of the Missouri School of Religion, for various assistances during the preparation of the dissertation.

I would like also to acknowledge the assistance of my wife, Myrna, who typed most of the dissertation.

INTRODUCTION

The primary purpose of this study is the structural analysis of the body of the Pauline letter. The study represents,
in the author's opinion, an additional step in the interpretation of the total form of the Pauline letter. The motivation
for the investigation stems from my belief that, when the structural components have been established with sufficient clarity,
we will be enabled to assess the relation of the parts to each
other, the import of the respective parts within the whole, and
the significance of the Pauline letter as a letter type within
the Hellenistic world. And, since the study is envisaged as one
more stage in the cumulative process, we may frame the investigation, at the start, in relation to the broader questions of
the literary analysis of the letter.

Unfortunately, the letter form has not been brought suffi-
ciently into view as a whole, in either the common letter tradition or in the New Testament letters, although not entirely
for the same reasons. Our knowledge of the common Greek letter,
for example, is dependent on the private Greek letters preserved
among the non-literary papyri. And, though roughly three-quar-
ters of a century has elapsed since the first major papyri finds,
most of the effort in papyrology has been devoted, necessarily,
to the editing and publication of the material. Apart from a
few excellent studies on the form and phraseology of various
kinds of documents, therefore, little has been done by the way
of thorough literary analysis.

With regard to the Pauline letters (and the New Testament
letters in general), literary analysis has lagged behind comparable advance in the Synoptic Gospels and Acts primarily because of the influence of one man, Adolf Deissmann. Deissmann
suggested that the form of the Pauline letter, apart from the
necessary epistolary conventions (i.e., salutation and closing),
like that of the common Greek letter of the day, was determined
by the needs of the moment.[1] We should expect the Pauline

---

[1]Adolf Deissmann, *Bible Studies,* A. Grieve, trans. (Edinburgh: T. & T. Clark, 1901), 3-59.

letters to be somewhat chaotic, therefore, since impromptu letter writing, according to Deissmann, has disorganization as its
natural concomitant.

A number of more recent literary analyses, however, both
of the common letter tradition and of the Pauline corpus, have
been demonstrating, little by little, that Deissmann's conception of the letter was inaccurate. We have hesitated, nonetheless, perhaps from force of habit as much as anything, to advance counter theses respecting the form of the letter. In any
case, the various style, form, and sequence analyses of smaller
units within the letter have adequately demonstrated the more
structural nature of the letter, and we may now work with the
larger structural units and with the letter form as a whole.
The amount of work to be done is very great, and division of
labor is a necessity. For this reason, I have confined myself
to the letter-body.

I propose to implement this study by means of three chapters, which represent successive steps in the total analysis.
The first chapter is the analysis of the phraseology, form, and
"idea" (function) of the letter-body in the private Greek letter. The second chapter is the analysis of the comparable aspects of the Pauline letter-body. The final chapter is a comparison of the body of the letter in Paul and in the common
letter tradition.

My primary object, as suggested at the outset, is the elucidation of the Pauline letter-body, and I employ the preceding
steps for the following reasons. Though I disagree with Deissmann's interpretation of the nature of the letter, he was on
the right track when he compared the Pauline letters to the private Greek letter. The common letter tradition, though certainly not the only tradition on which Paul depends, is the primary
literary *Gattung* to which the Pauline letters belong. In addition, since parallels have been established already between
other formal segments of the Pauline letter and the papyri, it
is appropriate to extend the comparison to the body. And the
letter-body of the private Greek letter is analyzed prior to
the corresponding unit in Paul, in order that new leverage may
be gained on the analysis of the Pauline letter-body. Concomitantly, the analysis of the private Greek letter provides an
appropriate basis for determining the nature and extent of dif-

ference between Paul and the common letter tradition. The third
chapter, in turn, functions as the conclusion, since the similarities and differences between Paul and the private Greek letter, implicit in the two preceding chapters, are taken up explicitly.

A number of relevant studies may be cited in connection
with the investigation of the letter form, but I consider it
more appropriate to take up these works, at relevant points,
in connection with the separate analyses of the common Greek
letter and the Pauline letter.

On the other hand, a few introductory qualifications regarding the study of the Pauline letter-body are necessary.
Seven letters will be subjected to formal analysis: Philemon,
Galatians, Romans, I and II Corinthians, I Thessalonians, and
Philippians. These seven letters were chosen because their
authenticity is generally accepted. And the letter-body of
Philemon, Galatians, and Romans, is analyzed as the first step
within the Pauline corpus, since the integrity of these letters is largely assumed. This number and order of letters is
proposed as a means of making the analysis of the Pauline
letter-body as objective as possible.

The body of the letter is treated separately in the common
letter tradition and in the Pauline letters. This procedure
commended itself as the one most likely to advert premature
assimilation of one body of data to the other.

The following suggestions are appropriate to the presentation of letters from the common letter tradition in the first
chapter. Dates are indicated thus: i, ii, and iii refer to
the first, second, or third century (the qualification B.C. or
A.D. immediately follows the preceding abbreviation); where a
particular year is indicated, it takes the following form:
157 B.C. or 37 A.D. The terms Ptolemaic, Roman, and Byzantine,
correspond to the following chronological periods: Ptolemaic,
from the third century B.C. to the time of Christ; Roman, from
the birth of Christ to 300 A.D.; and Byzantine, from the fourth
century A.D. on.

I have employed the customary abbreviations in references
to the papyri. Those instances of inaccurate accent and spell-
ing in the papyri are presented in uncorrected form. But, since
translation is customarily provided, the uncorrected forms should
not constitute a problem.

For the discussion of the Pauline letter-body, the translation of passages (unless otherwise specified) is from the Revised Standard Version of the Bible.

CHAPTER ONE

TRANSITIONAL FORMULAE IN NON-LITERARY PAPYRI LETTERS

Introduction

The three basic parts of the common Greek letter are:
opening; body; closing. The opening and closing formulae of
the common Greek letter were analyzed by F. X. J. Exler.[1] The
basic opening formulae, he suggested, in use throughout the
Ptolemaic and Roman periods were: A-to B- χαίρειν; To B-from
A-.[2] The basic closing formulae in use throughout these periods
were: ἔρρωσο (ἔρρωσθε), or its modifications; εὐτύχει later
changed into διευτύχει.[3] The letter parts characterized by
these formulae correspond, respectively, to our salutation and
farewell.

Conventional phrases in the body of the letter were also
analyzed by Exler but this segment of his work seems neither as
thorough nor as accurate as his analysis of the salutation and
farewell. He regarded the ἐρρῶσθαι wish, the ὑγιαίνειν wish,
and the ἀσπάσασθαι wish, for example, as initial phrases in the
body. Heikki Koskenniemi has examined these phrases and suggests that they, and other conventional phrases regarding the
addressee's welfare, are connected integrally with either the
opening or the closing of the letter.[4] Both the opening and
the closing are more extensive, therefore, than Exler assumed,
since the opening may contain (in addition to the salutation)
opening greetings; a health wish; a prayer formula (the *proskynema*-formula). The closing may contain a health wish and
closing greeting (as well as the farewell proper).

Exler's initial contribution plus the modifications by
Koskenniemi define the boundaries, in a back-handed way, of
the body of the letter, i.e., the body is that part which comes
immediately after opening conventions and immediately before
the closing formulae. A more positive description of the body
may be presented, however, despite its less homogeneous nature.[5]

The body, like the letter in general, may be divided into
three discrete sections: body-opening; body-closing; and section between opening and closing ("body-middle").

The transitions from letter-opening proper to the opening of the body, from body-opening to a new subject (i.e., the transition to the body-middle), or from the body-middle to body-closing, may often be identified by means of discrete transitional devices--both formulaic and non-formulaic. Some of these transitional constructions may be found in more than one body part; some have affinities with a certain body section; others are clearly confined to one specific section. These devices are both the means whereby the major body sections may be identified and also a means for tracking even minor body movements. The analysis of the nature of the body and the means whereby body-transitions are identified will proceed as outlined below.

Part A of this chapter (General Transitional Devices) is a study of the transitional phraseology (or language), formulaic and non-formulaic, which may be employed in more than one body-part. Each transitional category is introduced by a brief statement regarding the nature of that category, which is followed by actual examples from the non-literary papyri (arranged under body-part headings and generally according to chronology).

Each of the three major body-parts is characterized in part B by means of the transitional constructions specifically tied to one part of the body (Specific Transitional Constructions) and in the following sequence: the body-opening; the body-closing and the body-middle.[6]

The final section of the chapter, part C, is a summary of the means by which one may recognize transitions and it suggests also some criteria for differentiating major and minor transitions

A. General Transitional Devices in the Body

1. *Formulae.*

    a. Disclosure Formulae

    The transition from letter opening to opening of the body is made frequently by means of a "disclosure" formula, a formulaic phrase conveying either the addressor's desire or command that the addressee "know" something. The verb meaning "to know" appears frequently in stereotyped phrases throughout the body and seems to be employed generally for transitional purposes. Five discrete formulae employ the verb meaning "to know":

    (i) The full disclosure formula: γινώσκειν σε θέλω ὅτι...
    (ii) The imperative form: γίνωσκε ὡς or γίνωσκε ὅτι...

(iii) A motivation for writing: γέγραφα (οὖν) σοι ὅπως ἄν (or ἴνα) εἰδῇς.
(iv) The verb "to know" in the perfect indicative: οἶδες ὅτι ...or οἶδα ὅτι...
(v) The verb "to know" in the participial form (usually the perfect participle): εἰδώς (or εἰδότες) ὅτι...

Additional comments regarding both the nature of these disclosure formulae and the relative frequency of each within the separate body parts will be given following the examples.

Opening

(1) P.Mich.I 6,1   257 B.C.
οὐκ οἶμαι μέν σε ἀγνοεῖν περὶ 'Α. ὅτι...
"I think you are aware about Aischylos that..."[7]

(2) P.Mich.I 32,2ff.   255 B.C.
γνώριζε ἡμᾶς παραγεγενημένους νυνὶ ἐγ Μ.,...
"Know that I have now arrived from Memphis..."[8]

(3) P.Tebt.764,15ff.   185/161 B.C.
γίνωσκε τὰ "Ωρου κτήνη κατηνεχυρασμένα ὑπὸ τοῦ Πτολεμαίου φυλακίτου.
"Know that the animals of Horus have been taken in pledge by the guard of Ptolemaeus."

(4) P.Oxy.295,2ff.   ca 35 A.D.
γίνωσκε ὅτι Σελεύκος ἐλθὼν ὧδε πέφευγε.
"Know that Seleucus came here and has fled."[9]

(5) P.Giss.11,4   118 A.D.
γινώσκειν σε θέλω ὅτι...
"I want you to know that..."

(6) B.G.U.846,5f.   ii A.D.
γεινώσκειν σαι θέλω ὅτι...

(7) Class.Phil.xxii.p.243,4f.   ii A.D.
γεινώσκειν σε θέλω, μήτηρ, ὅτι...

(8) P.Bon.44,2f.   ii A.D.
γεινώσκειν σε θέλω ὅτι...

(9) P.Mert.83,2   late ii A.D.
γινώσκειν σε θέλω ὅτι...

(10) P.Fay.130,6   iii A.D.
γεινώσκιν σε θέλω, κύριέ μου, ὅτι...

(11) P.Bad.43,5f.   iii A.D.
γεινώσκειν σε θέλω, ἄδελφε, ὅτι...

(12) P.Oxy.1493,5f.   iii/iv A.D.
γινώσκειν σε θέλω, ἄδελφε, ὅτι...[10]

(13) P.Mich.10,2f.   257 B.C.
ὑπογέγραφά σοι τῆς παρὰ Σωσιπάτρου ἐλθούσης μοι ἐπιστολῆς τὸ ἀντίγραφον, ὅπως εἰδὼς ἀναφέρηις ἐν λόγωι 'Α.
"I have written for you below a copy of the letter which came to me from S., in order that you may take note and enter to the account of A."

(14) P.Tebt.746,1ff.   243 B.C.
τῆς παρὰ Μ. ἐπιστολῆς ὑπογέγραφά σοι τἀντίγραφα ὅπως εἰδῆις.
"I have written below for your information a copy of the letter from Menodorus."

(15) P.Oxy.1482,3   ii A.D.
γράφω σοι ἵν' ἰδῇς ὅτι...[11]

4

Closing

(16) P.Mich.10,13f.   257 B.C.
γέγραφα οὖν σοι ὅπως εἰδῇις.
"I wrote to you therefore in order that you
may know."
(17) P.Tebt.747,16f.   243 B.C.
ἔγραψα σοῦν σοι ἵνα εἰδῇις τὴν σαυτοῦ ἀμέλειαν.
(18) P.Par.43(=U.P.Z.66),4   154 B.C.
γέγραφ' ἱμεῖν ἵνα εἰδῆται.
(19) P.Oxy.299,5   late i A.D.
..., ἵνα εἰδῇς.
(20) P.Mich.512,6
διὸ γράφω σοι ἵν' εἰδῇς.
(21) P.Fay.129,8f.   iii A.D.
ἵν' οὖν ἰδῇς ἀναφέρω σοι.
(22) P.Beattv Panop.2,col.iv,133   300 A.D.
ὡς δ' ἂν εἰδείητε τὰ...

Body-Middle

(23) P.Mich.28,6f.   256 B.C.
γνώριζε οὐ δυνατὸν ὂν ἔτι.
"Know that it is no longer possible..."
(24) P.Mich.28,16   256 B.C.
γνώριζε οὖν...
(25) P.Tebt.315,10   ii A.D.
γείνωσκε γὰρ...
(26) P.Oxy.1067,6ff.   iii A.D.
μάθε οὖν ὅτι ἀλλοτρίαν γυναῖκον ἐκληρονόμησεν
αὐτόν.
"Know then that a strange woman is made his heir."
(27) P.Oxy.1589,10   iv. A.D.
γίνωσκε δὲ ὅτι...
(28) P.Oxy.743,27f.   2 B.C.
ὥστ' ἂν τοῦτο σε θέλω γεινώσκειν ὅτι...
"I wish you therefore to know this that..."
(29) P.Mich.203,5f.   reign Trajan
γεινώσκειν σε θέλω ὅτι...
(30) P.Oxy.1069,9ff.   iii A.D.
θέλω δὲ εἰδένε πῶς σπουδάδεις αὐτῶ γενέστε.
(31) P.S.I.1080,8   iii A.D.
εἰδέναι δέ σε θέλω ὅτι...
(32) P.Mich.28,7f.   256 B.C.
οὐκ εἴδοτες γὰρ διότι χρείαν ἕξεις
"For not being aware that you would be wanting it..."
(33) P.Tebt.409,8f.   5 A.D.
εἰδὼς ὅτι ἐξουσίαν αὐτῶν ἔχει καὶ Λυσίμαχος
καὶ σύ.
"..., for I know that both Lysimachus and you
had plenty of them."
(34) P.Oxy.1672,14ff.   37-41 A.D.
ἐπιγνοὺς οὖν τὸν παρὰ σοὶ ἀέρα ἱκανὸς ἔσῃ
περὶ πάντων.
"When then you have learnt how the wind is with
you, you will be able to judge of everything."
(35) P.Oxy.113,13f.   ii A.D.
γινώσκων ὅτι...

(36) P.Oxy.930,8ff.   ii/iii A.D.
ἡμερίμνουν γὰρ περὶ αὐτοῦ εἰδυῖα ὅτι κατὰ δύναμιν
μέλλει σοι προσέχειν.
"..., for I had no anxiety about him, knowing
that he intended to look after you to the best
of his ability."
(37) P.Fay.136,1   iv A.D.
...εἰδότες ὅτι
(38) P.Oxy.745,6   l A.D.
οὐκ οἶδας γὰρ πῶς μοι ἐχρήσατο ἐν Ὀξυρύγχοις...
"You do not know how he treated me at Oxyrhynchus..."
(39) P.Mich.203,28   reign Trajan
οἶδες ὅτι τί ἐὰν δῷς Ἰούλιω...
"You know that whatever you give Julius..."
(40) P.Mich.476,17   ii A.D.
σὺ δὲ οἶδες σατῷ πάλιν ὅτι...
"You are aware, for another thing, that..."
(41) B.G.U.846,10f.   ii A.D.
λοιπὸν οἶδα τί (ἐγὼ) αἰμαυτῷ παρέσχημαι.
"Well, I know what I brought on myself."
(42) P.Oxy.1219,11   iii A.D.
ἀλλὰ οἶδα ὅτι καὶ ταῦτα μου γράμματα...
"But I know that this letter of mine..."
(43) P.Tebt.424,3   iii A.D.
...καὶ εἴσως οἶδας τί σοι ἔγραψα.
"...and perhaps you know what I wrote you."

The body-opening commonly employs three disclosure forms:
the fuller form (i); the imperative form (ii); and the motivation for writing formula (iii). The fuller form (i) is predominant in private letters,[12] while the imperative form (ii)
and the motivation for writing formula (iii) are usually found
in business letters.[13] The perfect indicative (iv) and the
participial form (v) sometimes appear in the opening but their
number is negligible.[14] The closing of the body commonly
employs only one disclosure formula: the motivation for writing
formula (iii).[15] The section of the body between the opening
and the closing, on the other hand, employs all of the disclosure formulae except the motivation for writing form. The
perfect indicative and the participial form occur more often,
however, than the other two forms.[16]

    b. Expressions of Reassurance
    The body of the letter often contains a phrase of reassur-
ance concerning either the addressor's welfare; the addressor's
continued allegiance; or reassurance regarding some concrete
business matter. These expressions appear throughout the body
and usually in one of three forms. All three forms frequently
employ the subjunctive of prohibition.

(i) The verb νομίζω with the negative particle μή, occasionally the vocative, the conjunction ὅτι and the verb ἀμελέω.

(ii) The verb δοξάζω with the negative particle, the first person of the personal pronoun, and the perfect infinitive or participle of ἀμελέω.

(iii) Statements urging the addressee not to be anxious, though not as stereotyped as the preceding two forms, usually contain the adjective ἀμέριμνος (or the verb μεριμνάω with the negative particle) or the verb ἀγωνιάω with the negative particle.

Opening

(1) P.Mert.81,2f.   ii A.D.
μή με δόξῃς ἠμεληκέναι περί σου.
"Do not suppose that I have neglected you."

(2) P.Mich.206,11   ii A.D.
τοῦτο μὴ νομίσῃς ὅτι...
"Do not think that..."

(3) P.Tebt.315,7ff.   ii A.D.
καὶ νῦν δὲ μετὰ σπονδῆς γράφω ὅπως μὴ μεριμνῇς
"...and now I am writing in haste to prevent your being anxious."

(4) P.Oxy.1296,5ff.   iii A.D.
ἀμερίμνη οὖν, πάτερ, χάριν τῶν μαθημάτων ἡμῶν
"Now do not be uneasy, father, about my studies."

Closing

(5) P.Mich.18,3f.   257 B.C.
γεγράφαμέν σοι ἵνα εἰδὼς μὴ ἀγωνιαῖς.
"I have written you that you may know and not feel anxious."

(6) P.Oxy.1070,41f.   iii A.D.
τι ὑμεῖν περὶ αὐτῶν, ταχέως μοι δηλώσατε, ὃ τι
ἐὰν ἐπιδημῶν τοῖς ἐνθάδε οἷος ᾤμην ποιεῖν περὶ
τούτου μὴ ἀμελήσω.
"If therefore you meet and come to any conclusion about them let me know quickly, and anything that I thought I could do, being here, I will not neglect."

Body-Middle

(7) P.Oxy.1154,6f.   i A.D.
μὴ ἀγωνιάσῃς δὲ περὶ ἐμοῦ ὅτι...
"..., and do not be anxious about me because..."

(8) B.G.U.665,col.III,11ff.   i A.D.
μὴ δόξῃς ἀμελεῖν με τοῦ γράφειν σοι...
"Do not think I neglected to write you..."

(9) P.Oxy.530,7f.   ii A.D.
τὸ δὲ πραγμάτιον περὶ οὗ ἔγραψα Θ. μὴ μελέτω
σοι εἰ μὴ τετέλεσται.
"Do not be concerned that the matter about which I wrote to Theon has not been carried out..."

7

(10) P.Tebt.413,6f.   ii/iii A.D.
μὴ δόξῃς με, κυρία, ἠμεληκέναι σου τῶν ἐντολῶν.
"Do not think, sir, that I have neglected your
orders."
(11) P.Oxy.930,11ff.   ii/iii A.D.
ἐμέλησε δέ μοι πέμψαι καὶ πυθέσθαι περὶ τῆς
ὑγίας σου
"I took care to send and ask about your health..."
(12) P.Oxy.1493,9ff.   iii/iv A.D.
τούτου οὖν τὴν ἐπιμέλειαν ποιήσω ὡς ἰδίου υἱοῦ.
οὐκ ἀμελήσω δὲ ἀναγκάζειν αὐτὸν παραπροσέχειν
τῷ ἔργῳ,...
"I shall take care of him as if he were my own
son. I shall not neglect to make him attend to
his work,..."

Reassurance statements, as the examples are intended to
illustrate, are found infrequently in the closing.[17] They are
found most often in the body-middle, marking a transition to
a new subject.[18] They must usually be considered, therefore,
a transition of major rank in the body-middle.

   c. "Responsibility" Statements
   The addressor frequently summons the addressee to be concerned, or not to be neglectful, about something within the
body of the letter. Two distinct formulae, utilizing the verbs
ἀμελέω and μέλω, recur throughout the body; one of the verbs
(ἀμελέω) is frequently a subjunctive of prohibition (like reassurance statements).

                        Opening

(1) P.Mich.201,4ff.   99 A.D.
καλῶς ὃν ποιήσαται μελήσαιτε ἡμῖν περὶ τῶν...
"Please be so good as to take thought about the..."
(2) P.Tebt.415,3f.   ii A.D.
καλῶς ποιήσις μὴ ἀμελήσις περὶ...
"You will do well not to neglect the..."[19]
(3) P.Mert.85,5f.   mid iii A.D.
γράφων περὶ τῆς σωτηρίας σου, ἄδελφε, μὴ ἀμέλει.
"Do not be negligent in writing about your health,
my brother."
(4) P.Amh.143,2f.   iv A.D.
μὴ ἀμελήσῃς ἐν τῇ αὔριον ἀπαντῆσαι πρὸς ἡμᾶς
"Do not neglect to come and meet us tomorrow,..."

8

Closing

(5) P.S.I.499,7   257/6 B.C.
παραγενοῦ δὲ καὶ αὐτὸς καὶ μὴ ἄλλως ποιήσηις. [20]
"Also, make sure that you come up."

(6) P.Tebt.767,11f.   ii B.C.
εἰ δ' ἄλλως ποήσεις ἐσῇ πάντας ἡμᾶς λελυπηκώς.
"If you do otherwise, you will annoy us all."

(7) P.Oxy.745,7f.   *ca* 1 A.D.
ἐρωτῶ οὖν σε μὴ ἄλλως ποῆσαι,...
"I request you, therefore, not to do otherwise,..."

(8) P.Fay.119,23f.   *ca* 100 A.D.
μὴ οὖν ἄλλος πυήσῃς.

(9) P.Oxy.742,14f.   2 B.C.
μὴ ἀμελήσῃς. ἔρρωσο.
"Do not neglect. Good-bye."

(10) B.G.U.1031,11f.   ii A.D.
ἀλλ' ὅρα μὴ ἀμελήσῃς τὸν...
"But see that you do not neglect the..."

(11) P.S.I.1260,29   iii A.D.
ἀλλ' ὅρα μὴ ἀμελήσῃς.

(12) P.Oxy.930,18ff.   ii/iii A.D.
ὥστε οὖν, τέκνον, μελησάτω σοί τε καὶ τῷ
παιδαγωγῷ...
"So now, my child, you and your attendant must
take care..."

(13) P.Ryl.241,7ff.   iii A.D.
καὶ μελησάτω σοι περὶ ὧν σοι ἐνετίλατο Σωκράτης.
"...and be careful of the order which Socrates
gave you."

Body-Middle

(14) P.S.I.516,2f.   251/0 B.C.
μελησάτω δέ σοι...
"But let it be a concern to you..."

(15) P.Amh.131,8f.   early ii A.D.
μελησάτω σοι ὅπως ἀγορασθῇ τὰ κενώματα...
"See that the empty jars are bought,..."

(16) P.S.I.1241,22ff.   159 A.D.
περὶ τῶν ἔργων τοῦ ἀμπελῶνος, ὡς ἐνετειλάμην
ὑμεῖν, μὴ ἀμελήσητε,...
"Regarding the work of the vineyard, do not be
neglectful, just as I ordered you..."

(17) P.Tebt.419,5f.   iii A.D.
ὅρα μὴ ἀμελήσῃς

(18) P.Mich.219,11f.   296 A.D.
ἐπιμέλετε δὲ
"Take serious thought..."[21]

    Responsibility phrases open the body relatively often (exx.
1-4); are slightly more frequent in the body-middle (exx. 14-
18); and especially prevelant in the body-closing (exx. 5-13).
The body-closing not only employs the two verbs previously cited
in connection with such phrases (i.e., ἀμελέω, exx. 9-11; and

μέλω, exx. 12 and 13), but at least three additional constructions, only one of which (the phrase μή οὖν ἄλλως ποιήσῃς, exx.
5-8) is listed here. A more extensive treatment of responsibility phrases in the body-closing, and the nuances associated with
such phrases there, will be presented separately in part B of
this chapter.

    d. "Grief" (or "Anxiety") Expressions
    Various expressions of grief, anxiety, and alarm are found
intermittently, either opening the body or occurring in the
body-middle. One grief (or anxiety) form alone, however, seems
to recur commonly as a discrete formula. The following items
are often included: (i) the verb ἀκούω (or ἐπιγινώσκω) usually in
the participial form; (ii) the object of the report stated by
various grammatical constructions; (iii) the verb λυπέω (or
ἀγωνιάω in the aorist active form) in the aorist passive form;
(iv) the adverb λίαν (or σφόδρα or some other surrogate for
denoting the degree of grief).[22]

Opening

(1) P.S.I.333,1ff.   256 B.C.
    συνέβη ἡμῖν ἀγωνιᾶσαι ἀκούσαντας ἐπὶ πλείονα
    χρόνον ἐλκυσθῆναί σε ἐν ἀρρωστίαι, νυνὶ δὲ
    ἀκούσαντές σε ὑγιαίνειν καὶ εἶναι ἤδη...
    "I suffered anxiety when I heard of your pro-
    tracted illness, but now I am delighted to hear
    that you are convalescent and already on the
    point of recovery."
(2) P.Giss.19,3f.   ii A.D.
    μεγάλως ἀγωνιῶσα περί σου διὰ τὰ ὄντα τοῦ
    καιποῦ φημιζόμενα...
    "I agonized greatly concerning you because of
    what is presently rumored..."
(3) P.Giss.17,5ff.   ii A.D.
    ἠγωνίασα, κύριε, οὐ μετρίως ἵνα ἀκούσω ὅτι
    ἐνώθρευσας, ἀλλὰ χάρις τοῖς θεοῖς πᾶσι ὅτι
    σε διαφυλάσσουσι ἀπρόσκοπον.
    "I was distressed, my lord, not a little to
    hear that you had been ill, but thanks be to
    all the gods that they keep you safe from harm."
(4) B.G.U.449,4f.   ii/iii A.D.
    ἀκούσας ὅτι νωθρεύῃ ἀγωνιοῦμεν...
    "I am anxious because I heard you were ill..."
(5) P.Oxy.930,4f.   ii/iii A.D.
    ἐλοιπήθην ἐπιγνοῦσα παρὰ...
    "I was grieved to learn from (the daughter of
    our teacher D. that he had gone down the river.)"

Body-Middle

(6) P.Tebt.760,20ff.   215/14 B.C.
ἀκούσας δὲ τὰ κατὰ τὸν Πτολεμαῖον ἐλυπήθην σφόδρα.
"I was deeply grieved to hear about the case of
Ptolemaeus."

(7) P.Oxy.1676,10f.   iii A.D.
ἀλλὰ λείαν ἐλυπήθην ὅτι οὐ παραγένου...
"But I was very much grieved that you did not
come..."

(8) P.Amh.145,15ff.   iv/v A.D.
γνῶθει δὲ ὅτι ἐλυπήθην διότι ἀπεδήμησας ἀλόγως...
αὐτή ἐστιν ἡ συνταγή, ἀλλ᾽ ἐχάρην ἀκούσας διὰ τοῦ
πραιποσίτου ὅτι ἀπέρχη ταχυτέρου πρὸς ἡμᾶς.
"Know that I am grieved because you went away
without cause..., but I rejoice at hearing
through the Praepositus that you are soon coming
back to us."

2. *Non-formulaic Transitional Devices*

a. Receipt and Transfer Statements

John Winter made the simple but important observation that
Egypt, at the time of the writing of the papyri, as now, was
predominantly an agricultural country and that farm work was
naturally one of the commonest topics of letters and documents.[23]
The sending and receiving of supplies is, therefore, a common
topic within the body of the papyri letter. Such statements
may appear in all three designated body parts but are found
only rarely in the body-closing and, apart from business letters,
only slightly more often in the body-opening. Notifications
of receipt or transfer are primarily characteristic, therefore,
of the body-middle. The same verbs are regularly employed: if
reference is to receipt, the verbs κομίζω and λαμβάνω occur;
if the reference is to transfer, the verbs are πέμπω or
ἀποστέλλω.

Opening

(1) P.Hib.41,2ff.   *ca* 261 B.C.
ἀπεστάλκαμεν πρὸς σὲ Μνάσωνα τὸν δοκιμαστὴν
μετὰ φυλακῆς.
"I have sent to you Mnason the controller
under guard."

(2) P.Oxy.293,3ff.   27 A.D.
οὐδεμίαν μοι φᾶσιν ἀπέστειλας περὶ τῶν ἱματίων...
"You have sent me no word about the clothes..."

(3) P.S.I.841,2ff.   iv A.D.
ἀπέστιλά σοι τὸν ἀδελφόν μου...
"I sent my brother to you..."

(4) P.Tebt.289,3   23 A.D.
    ἐξαυτῆς πέμπε μοι πρόσγραφον...
    "Send me at once a statement..."
(5) P.Fay. 113,3f.   100 A.D.
    πάντη πάντος πέμσις Πίνδαρον...
    "Make all haste to send Pindar..."
(6) P.Mich.28,1f.   256 B.C.
    ἐκομισάμην τὴν παρὰ σοῦ ἐπιστολήν...
    "I received your letter..."
(7) P.Oxy.1293,4f.   117-38 A.D.
    κόμισαι παρὰ Σαρᾶτος Μάρκον...
    "Receive from Saras' son Marcus..."

Closing

(8) P.Hib.43,8ff.   261/60 B.C.
    (ἵνα οὖν μηθὲν ὑστερῆι τὰ ἐλαιουργία φρόντισον
    ἵνα μὴ αἰτίας ἔχῃς) καὶ τοὺς ἐλαιουργοὺς
    ἀποστειλόν μοι. ἔρρωσο.
    "(Take care then that the oil-presses do not fall
    short, lest you be blamed;) and send me the oil-
    makers. Good-bye."
(9) P.Oxy.1155,11ff.   104 A.D.
    αὐτὸ τὸ πρόγραμμα τοῦ ἡγεμόνος ἔπεμψά σοι ἵνα
    ἐπίγοις πρὸς τί σοί ὅτι. ἔρρωσο.
    "I send you the actual proclamation of the prae-
    fect that you may hasten to do what concerns you.
    Good-bye."

Body-Middle

(10) P.S.I,349,5   254/3 B.C.
     ἀπεστάλκαμεν δὲ περὶ τούτου...
     "And we have sent about this..."
(11) P.S.I.783,6f.   357 A.D.
     καὶ ἀπόστιλον διὰ τῶν αὐτῶν...
     "And send by the same means..."
(12) P.Mich.203,22f.   reign Trajan
     καλῶς ποιήσεις πέμψον ᾽Ι. ...
     "Please send to J. ..."
(13) P.Oxy.1293,23f.   117-138 A.D.
     ἔπεμψα ᾽Απολλωνίωι τῶι ἀδελφῷ εἰς Βαφὴν ἐρίδια,...
     "I sent my brother Apollonius some wool for
     dying,..."
(14) P.Oxy.1479,2   late i B.C.
     ἐκομισάμην τὸ ἐπιστόλιον Θρασυβούλου...
     "I received the letter of Thrasybulus..."
(15) P.Tebt.413,9f.   ii/iii A.D.
     καὶ κομίση δι᾽ ᾽Αρτήους καὶ τὸ φοροχίον...
     "Receive through Artes (?) the hold-all..."
(16) P.Mert.85,8f.   mid iii A.D.
     κόμισαι παρὰ τοῦ ἀναδιδόντος σοι τὰ γράμματα
     "Receive (22 pairs of small wheat-loaves) from
     him who delivers the letter to you."

The preceding examples were intended to reflect the following characteristics of transfer and receipt statements:

(i) Transfer statements (exx. 1-5 and 8-13 here) are generally found more often than receipt statements (exx. 6-7 and 14-16).

(ii) ἀποστέλλω is frequent in the third century B.C., represented above by examples 1, 8, and 10, and in the fourth century A.D., represented by examples 3 and 11, but rare in other periods.[24]

(iii) Receipt and transfer statements are rarely found in the body-closing (exx. 8-9), and when they do appear they should usually be regarded as a postscript.[25]

b. References to Writing

The reference to writing occurs regularly throughout the body of the letter. The non-formulaic nature of such references-- apart from the "motivation for writing" form of the disclosure formula and a few other stereotyped phrases to be presented later in connection with specific body sections--prohibits judgment, however, on the possible transitional function of these statements. A few examples from each body section are illustrated below in order to call attention to the possible importance of such statements.

Opening

(1) P.Mich.36,1f.   254 B.C.
     ἔγραψας ἡμῖν ὅτι Παῖς...
     "You wrote us that Pais..."
(2) P.Oxy.297,3f.   54 A.D.
     καλῶς ποιήσεις γράψεις διὰ πιττακίων...
     "Kindly write me in a note..."
(3) P.Oxy.1068,4f.   iii A.D.
     ἔγραψα τῷ κυρίῳ μου Κ. τῷ ἀρχιερῖ εἶνα...
     "I wrote to my lord Clematius the chief priest
     that..."

Closing

(4) P.Mich.58,29f.   248 B.C.
     γράψον οὖν ἐν τάχει περὶ τούτων.
     "Write therefore in haste about these things."
(5) B.S.A.A.xiv.p.194,10f.   i B.C.
     γέγραφαν δὲ ὑμεῖν καὶ οἱ ἀπ' Ἀλεξ. στολισταὶ
     περὶ αὐτοῦ.
     "The Stolistae of Alexandria have also written
     to you about him."

(6) Class.Phil.xxii.p.243,13f.   ii A.D.
     καὶ ᾿γὼ εἴ τινα ἐὰν εὕρω γράφω σοι; οὐ μὴ
     ὀκνήσω σοι γράφιν.
     "And whenever I find a messenger I will write
     to you; never will I be slow to write."

Body-Middle

(7) P.Oxy.1757,19   ii A.D.
     γράψον μοι ἐπιστολὴν διὰ...
     "Write me a letter through..."
(8) B.G.U.846,9f.   ii A.D.
     αἴγραψά σοι ὅτι γυμνός εἴμει.
     "I wrote to you that I am naked."
(9) P.Oxy.1160,12f.   iv A.D.
     γράψον μοι εἴνα...
     "Write to me that..."

c. Grammatical Constructions

A few grammatical constructions are commonly employed for
transitional purposes within the body. Three of these constructions are regularly found in at least two of the three
body-sections: conditional clauses; the vocative; περί with
the genitive.

i. *Conditional Clauses*--Conditional clauses are frequent
both in the body-closing and in the body-middle. They are
rarely employed, on the other hand, to open the body. The form
most often encountered in the papyri is the future protasis
with ἐάν and the subjunctive.[26]

Conditions are regularly employed with a specific nuance
only in the body-closing. Their meaning there will be taken
up subsequent to the presentation of examples.

Opening

(1) P.Flor.162,2ff.   *ca* 260 A.D.
     εἴ τι δύνασε τῶν μετρημάτων, παράδος τῷ
     δεκαπρώτῳ διὰ τοῦ σοῦ σιτομέτρου...
     "Deliver any corn-dues that you can to the
     decemprimus through your corn-measurer..."
(2) P.Mert.32,2ff.   iv A.D.
     μέχρι σήμορον ἐγὼ πίστις σοι ἀπεπλήρωσα διὰ
     τὴν μητερά σου; ἰ μὲν οὖν ἀσφαλῶς βούλη αὐτὼ
     ὀνήσασσται δός τι ἀπὸ μέρους τῇ Λιβικῇ δυαὶ
     ἀνθρώπων.
     "Up to today I have, with the help of your
     mother, discharged the pledges on your behalf.
     If then you wish to make sure of buying it,
     give an installment to Libike through her
     servants.

Closing

(3) Hib.42,8f.   262/61 B.C.
ἐὰμ μὴ μεταβάληις ἕως Ἀθὺρ η δώσομεν Λευκίωι
ἐν ὀφειλήματι. ἔρρωσο.
"If you do not transfer before Athur 8, we shall
give to Leucius as a debt. Good-bye."

(4) P.Mich.21,7f.   257 B.C.
...ἐὰν οὖν μὴ ταχέως ἐπισκέψηι νοχλεῖσθαι τοῖς
ἵπποις.
"...so if you do not take thought at once, the
horses will be falling ill."

(5) P.Mich.204,7f.   127 A.D.
εἰ δ' ἄρα μὴ ἐκξέρχομαι ἀπ' αὐτῶν εἶτα καθ'
ἡμέρα δέρουσί με.
"For if I do not get away from them, then they
will give me a hiding every day."

(6) P.Fay.124,19ff.   ii A.D.
καὶ νῦν οὖν εἰ μὴ πίθῃ καὶ τὴν χορηγίαν τῇ
μητρὶ εὐγνομώνως ἀποδίδυς τὸ ἀκόλουθον τούτων
ἔσται καὶ μετάμελόν σοι πάλειν εἰσοίσει ἡ
πλεονεξία σου.
"...if you do not comply and pay your mother
her allowance in a fair manner, the consequences
of your behavior will follow and your cupidity
will again cause you regret."

(7) P.Tebt.424,6ff.   late iii A.D.
ἴσθι δὲ ὅτι ὀφίλις φόρους καὶ ἀποφορὰς ἑπτὰ
ἐτῶν, ὡς ἐὰν μὴ ἀποκαταστασίας μὴ πέμψῃς οἶδάς
σου τὸν κίνδυνον.
"Let me tell you that you owe seven years' rents
and dues, so unless you now send discharges you
know your danger."

(8) P.Mert.29,6ff.   iv A.D.
εἰ δ' οὖν τούτων ἀμελήσατε ὑμῖς ὑπὲρ αὐτοῦ
λόγον δώσετε.
"If you are negligent herein, you will be held
responsible for him."

Body-Middle

(9) P.Mich.14,2f.   257 B.C.
ἐὰν οὖν κομίσηι ἀπόστειλον ἡμῖν,...
"So if you receive them, send them to us..."

(10) P.Oxy.1153,18f.   i A.D.
ἀβόλλην σοι ἐὰν εὕρω ἀγοράσαι ἰδιωτικῶς ἐν
τάχει πέμψω,...
"If I can buy a cloak for you privately, I
will send it at once,..."

(11) P.Mich.203,7f.   reign Trajan
ἐὰν εὕρω εὐκαιρείαν...ἔρχομαι μετ' ἐπιστολῶν
πρὸς ὑμᾶς.
"If I find an opportunity (of putting my plan
into effect) I am coming to you with letters."

(12) J.E.A.xiii.p.61,27f.   293 A.D.
ἐὰν εὕρητε εὐκερίαν, μετὰ ἀνθρώπων καλῶν δεῦτε.
"If you find opportunity, come in good company."

Conditional clauses in the body-opening are even more rare than the two examples (1 and 2) suggest. They are simply not characteristic of that part of the body. Conditions in the body-middle and the body-closing, on the other hand, are more frequent than the examples suggest. They are employed with a variety of meaning in the body-middle and thus indicate transitional force in a variety of ways. Though they sometimes mark a major movement to a new subject, more often they are used for minor shifts, i.e., the transition to a new but minor subject or to the development of the present subject. Conditions in the body-closing, however, serve a rather uniform and major function. They almost always refer back to an important and earlier matter within the body (especially requests and commands) and function as the means of forcefully urging the addressee to pay attention to that matter.[27]

ii. *The Vocative*--The vocative is employed intermittently, during the Roman period, as a means of making major transitions in all three body-sections. The vocative case was also employed in the Ptolemaic period, but was confined almost entirely to the request section of letters of petition.[28] The vocative is also frequent in private letters of request, during the Roman period, but its use is extended, in addition, to all the points in the body where major transitions occur.

Opening

(1) Class.Phil.xxii.p.243,4f.   ii A.D.
γεινώσκειν σε θέλω, μήτηρ, ὅτι ἐρρώμενος
ἐγενόμην εἰς 'Ρώμην...
"I want you to know, mother, that I arrived at Rome in good health..."

(2) P.Fay.125,3ff.   ii A.D.
καλῶς ποιήσεις, ἄδελφε, μὴ ἀμελήσας τοῦ κλήρου
τοῦ στρατηγικοῦ,...
"You will do well, brother, not to neglect the ballot for the strategus,..."

(3) P.Mich.206,4f.   ii A.D.
φανερόν σοι ποιῶ, ἄδελφε,...
"I make known to you, brother,..."

(4) B.G.U.276,7ff.   ii/iii A.D.
παρακλήσεις, κύριέ μου ἄδελφε, λάβων τὰ
γράμματα Σερήνου...
"I entreat you, my lord brother, that when you receive Serenus' letters..."

(5) P.Oxy.1678,3ff.   iii A.D.
μὴ νομείσῃς, κύρειά μου μήτρη, ὅτει ἠμέλησα...
"Do not think, my lady mother, that I neglected..."

Closing

(6) Rev.Eg.1919.p.204,28f.   ii A.D.
ταῦτά σοι ἔγραψα, ἄδελφε, ἐπειστάμενος...
"This I have written to you, brother, because
I know..."

(7) P.Oxy.930,18f.   ii/iii A.D.
ὥστε οὖν, τέκνον, μελησάτω σοί τε καὶ...
"So now, my child, you and..."

(8) P.Warren 20,4ff.   iii A.D.
καὶ αὐτὸς οὖν, κύριέ μου Πάτρων, περὶ ὧν βούλει,
κέλευέ μοι,...
"Yourself also, my lord Patron, order me about
whatever you like,..."

Body-Middle

(9) P.Enteuxeis 82,6   220 B.C.
δέομαι οὖν σου, βασιλεῦ, εἴ σοι δοκεῖ,...
"I entreat you therefore, king, if you approve,..."

(10) P.Tebt.409,10f.   5 A.D.
σὲ δὲ ἠρώτησα, φίλτατέ μου, εἰδὼς ὅτι...
"I asked you, dear friend, since I know that..."

(11) B.G.U.846,10   ii A.D.
παρακαλῶ σαι, μῆτηρ, διαλάγητί μοι.
"I beg you, mother, be reconciled to me."

(12) P.Flor.338,9f.   iii A.D.
ὥστε, ἄδελφε, σπούδασον;...
"So, brother, exert yourself;..."

(13) P.Oxy.1666,17   iii A.D.
μελησάτω σοι οὖν, ἄδελφε, περὶ τοῦ γράμματος
τῆς ὑποθήκης...
"So, brother, take charge yourself of the deed
of mortgage,..."

   iii.   Περί *with the Genitive*--Περί with the genitive is
often shorthand in private correspondence for: "to a subject
mentioned in previous communication." Whether in tandem with
a stereotyped formula or in a non-formulaic clause, περί frequently denotes a matter of previous communication (the reference is either to a previous occasion or to an earlier matter
in the body) in all three sections.

Opening

(1) P.Hib.40,2ff.   261 B.C.
περὶ τῶν συμβόλων γεγράφαμεν Κρίτωνι καὶ
Καλλικλεῖ,...
"I have written Criton and Callicles about the
receipts,..."

(2) P.Mich.201,4ff.   99 A.D.
     καλῶς ὂν ποιήσαται μελήσαιτε ἡμῖν περὶ τῶν...
     "Please be so good as to take thought about the..."
(3) P.Oxy.530,2ff.   ii A.D.
     περὶ ὧν μοι γράφεις ἐπιστολὴν πασῶν ἐκομισάμην...
     "I have received all the letters about which
     you write,..."
(4) P.Tebt.423,2ff.   iii A.D.
     καὶ ἀλλοτέσοι ἔγραψα ὑπομιμνήσκων περὶ τῶν...
     "I have written to you on other occasions to
     remind you about the work..."

                        Closing

(5) B.S.A.A.xiv.p.194,10f.   i B.C.
     γέγραφαν δὲ ὑμεῖν καὶ οἱ ἀπ' Ἀλεξανδρείας
     στολισταὶ περὶ αὐτοῦ.
     "The stolistae of Alexandria have also written
     to you about him."
(6) P.Amh.135,17ff.   ii A.D.
     περὶ τῶν κεραμίων τῆς θαλλοῦ μελησάτω σοι ὅπως
     ἐκξωδιασθῇ...
     "Concerning the jars for the festivities, see
     that they are paid..."
(7) P.Oxy.1220,23ff.   iii A.D.
     καὶ περὶ τῶν χωρίων, ἐὰν παραγένῃ σὺν θεῷ,
     μαθήσι τὴν διάθησιν αὐτῶν.
     "About the fields, if you come, god willing, you
     will learn the condition."

                      Body-Middle

(8) P.Mich.55,11f.   240 B.C.
     ἔγραψα δέ σοι καὶ περὶ Ἑρμοκράτου πρότερον,...
     "I wrote you once before about Hermokrates,..."
(9) P.Mich.201,9f.   99 A.D.
     καὶ ἐρωτήσαται Ἀ. περὶ τῶν...
     "And ask Apion about the..."
(10) P.S.I.1241,22ff.   159 A.D.
     περὶ τῶν ἔργων τοῦ ἀμπελώνος, ὡς ἐνετειλάμην
     ὑμεῖν, μὴ ἀμελήσητε,...
     "Do not neglect the work of the vineyard, just
     as I ordered you..."
(11) P.Oxy.930,8ff.   ii/iii A.D.
     ἡμερίμνουν γὰρ περὶ αὐτοῦ εἰδυῖα ὅτι...
     "...,for I had no anxiety about him, knowing
     that..."

     B.   Specific Transitional Devices

1.   *Body-Opening*

     The transition from the opening of the letter to the body-
opening is a major transition. The significance of the body-

opening is signalled by the frequency with which stereotyped
formulae open the body. Even when non-formulaic transitional
devices are employed, e.g., the vocative and περί with the
genitive, they often combine syntactically with a formula. It
will prove helpful, at this point, to illustrate the transition
from the letter-opening to the body-opening by means of an
actual letter.

letter-opening:	Ἀπολινάρις Ταῆσι τῇ μητρεῖ καί κυρίᾳ πολλὰ χαίρειν. πρὸ μὲν πάντων εὔχομαί σε ὑγειαίνειν, κἀγὼ αὐτὸς ὑγειαίνω καὶ τὸ προσκύνημά σου ποιῶ παρὰ τοῖς ἐνθάδε θεοῖς.
body-opening:	γεινώσκειν σε θέλω, μήτηρ, ὅτι ἐρρώμενος ἐγενόμην εἰς Ῥώμην Παχὼν μηνὶ κε καὶ ἐκληρώθην εἰς Μισηνούς,...(This letter is example 1 on p. 15, Class.Phil.xxii)
letter-opening:	"Apollinarius to Taesis, his mother and lady, many greetings. Before all I pray for your health. I myself am well and make supplication for you before the gods of this place.
body-opening:	I wish you to know, mother, that I arrived in Rome in good health on the 25th of the month Pachan and was posted to Misenum,..."

The opening of this letter, as is customary, is introduced
by the salutation. The salutation in turn is succeeded by a
health wish and a prayer formula which, in this instance, are
syntactically combined.[29] Immediately following the prayer
formula, the body-opening is introduced by the fuller form (i)
of the disclosure formula. The major transitional significance
of the disclosure formula in this letter is accentuated by the
use of the vocative, μήτηρ, which combines syntactically with
the formula.

Both the disclosure formula and the vocative of the preceding letter were analyzed as "general transitional devices"
in section A. In addition to these constructions, we find
transitional formulae specifically tied to the body-opening.
Before turning to the examination of such formulae, however,
we may provisionally define the nature and function of the
body-opening.

The body-opening is the point at which the principal occasion for the letter is usually indicated. In addition,

the body-opening must proceed, like spoken conversation, from a
basis common to both parties. This is provided either by allu-
sion to subject matter shared by both parties or by the addressor's disclosure of new information. The body-opening lays the
foundation, in either case, from which the superstructure may
grow.

The preceding definition is something of an index for determining which kinds of formulae are appropriate to open the body.
Not only are body-opening transitions usually formulaic, they
must also posit a base common to the two parties in the epistolary situation. We often encounter the fuller disclosure formula (i) and the περί with the genitive construction, for example,
because they supply this common base, either by imparting new
information or by referring back to previous matters shared by
both. Conditional clauses and responsibility statements are
found less often opening the body, on the other hand, because
in the papyri they are usually contingent on statements made
earlier in the body. Having sketched the principal characteristics of the body-opening, we may now turn to the transitional
constructions specifically connected with it.

a. Requests

The request is common in all parts of the body, but each
body-section has a few set types, in addition to the unspecified
requests, which may appear throughout. I have been able to
identify the following as body-opening requests because of the
phraseology integrally tied to them.

i. *Request for a Letter*--Reproach for failure to write is
a common means of opening the body. The following two patterns
usually function as the means whereby the reproach is stated.
The addressor either states the number of letters he has written
and then accentuates this number by contrasting it with the
addressee's failure to write, or he simply emphasizes the addressee's failure. The latter complaints are often introduced by
the first person of the verb θαυμάζω, accompanied by the vocative
or some other form of exclamatory address.

Complaints regarding failure to write bear little, if any,
formal resemblance to the background portion of the petition.
They function as a background, nonetheless, but as the specific

background to the request for a letter. The actual request, more often than not, is not stated, but the nature of the complaint itself and the explicit request in several letters indicate that such opening complaints signal a request for a letter. The letter-opening, succeeded by the body-opening request for a letter and its background (the complaint regarding failure to write), may be illustrated with the following letter.

> Σατορνῖλος Σεμπρωνίῳ τῷ ἀδελφῶι καὶ κυρίῳ πλεῖστα χαίρειν. πρὸ μὲν πάντων εὔχομέ σαι ὑγειένειν καὶ προκόπτειν, ἅμα δὲ καὶ τὸ προσκύνημά σου ποιοῦμε ἡμερησίως παρὰ τοῖς πατρῴες θεοῖς.
> θαυμάζω, ἀδελφε, δευτέραν ἐπιστολὴν αὕτη ἣν ἔπεμψά σοι ἀφ᾽ ἧς ἐγανάμην ἰς οἶκον καὶ οὐδεμίαν ἀντιφώνησίν μοι ἔπεμψας. ἐρωτηθεὶς οὖν, ἀδελφε, τάχιόν μοι γράφιν...30

> "Saturnilus to Sempronius, his brother and lord, very many greetings. Before all things I pray for your health and success; at the same time I also make daily obeisance for you before our ancestral gods.
> I wonder, brother—this is the second letter which I have sent to you since I came home, and you have written me no reply. I therefore ask you, brother, to write me at once..." (P.Mich.209,ii/iii A.D.)

The letter-opening has, respectively, the salutation, health-wish, and prayer formula. Immediately following the last item of the letter-opening (the prayer formula), the body-opening is indicated by the formulaic statement of complaint. The complaint about failure to write—expressed by the verb θαυμάζω, reference to the *number* of letters the addressor has written, and accentuation of the addressee's failure to write—is followed, in turn, by the explicit request for a letter. Once again the vocative (ἀδελφε here) accompanies the body-opening formula, further emphasizing the transitional significance of the body-opening. Additional examples of formulaic complaints (regarding failure to write) opening the body are illustrated below.

(1) B.G.U.1079,2f.   41 A.D.
    ἔπεμψά σοι ἄλλας δύο ἐπιστολάς,...
    "I sent you two other letters,..."
(2) Rev.Eg.1919.p.204,6ff.   ii A.D.
    τοσαύτας ὑμεῖν ἐπιστολὰς διεπεμψάμην κοὐδεμείαν
    μοι ἀντεγράψαται, τοσούτων καταπλευσάντων.
    "How many letters have I sent you and not one
    have you written in reply, though so many have
    sailed down!"

(3) P.Mich.484,3ff.   ii A.D.
ἤδη σοι ταύτην τρίτην ἐπιστολὴν γράφω καὶ σοί
μοι οὐδεμίαν ἀντιφώνησιν ἔπεμψες,...
"This is now the third letter I am writing you
and you have sent me no reply,..."

(4) P.Oxy.1216,4ff.   ii/iii A.D.
καὶ ἀπὸ μικρόθεν σὺ οἶδάς μου τὴν προαίρεσιν
κἂν μή σοι γράφω, σὺ δαὶ οὐκ ἠξίωσάς μαι ἀσπάσασθε
δι᾿ ἐπιστωλῆς.
"..., and you know from close experience my good-
will even though I do not write you; but you have
never thought proper to send me greetings in a letter."

(5) P.Mich.221,4ff.   296 A.D.
ἤδη ὀκτὼ μῆνες ἀφ᾿ ἦ εἰσῆλθα εἰς ᾿Αλεξ., οὐδὲ
μίαν μοι ἐπιστολὴν ἔγραψας.
"It is already eight months since I came to
Alexandria, and not even one letter have you
written."

(6) Rev.Eg.1919.p.201,6f.   iii A.D.
ἰδοὺ πέμπτον σοι τοῦτο γράφω, καὶ σοὶ εἰ μὴ
ἅπαξ μόνον οὐκ ἔγραψάς μοι...
"Look you, this is my fifth letter to you, and
you have not written to me except only once,..."[31]

     ii. *Request for the Addressee to Visit*--The request for
the addressee to visit or that he send someone (something) to
the addressor is a relatively frequent subject of the body-
opening. Such requests tend to have a stereotyped form, often
including the following three elements: (1) the reception of
the letter phrase; (2) a verb of coming or sending (usually in
the imperative mood); and (3) either a threat phrase (a) if
the recipient does not obey the request, or (b) an additional
request that the addressee bring something with him when he
comes.[32] The request for a visit (or for the addressee to
send someone) does not always introduce the body-opening. When-
ever any material is prior, however, it is usually background
material delineating the occasion for the request and hence
the request indicates the body-opening.[33]

(1) P.Hib.45,3ff.   257/56 B.C.
ὡς ἂν λάβητε τὴν ἐπιστολὴν παραγίνεσθε ἵνα...
"As soon as you receive this letter, come here
in order that..."

(2) P.Tebt.713,4ff.   ii B.C.
ὡς ἂν ἀναγνῶτε τὴν ἐπιστολήν μου, μηθὲν
στραγγευσάμενοι παραγένεσθε ἐν τάχει εἰς
᾿Οξύρυγχα. ...
"As soon as you read my letter, repair quickly
with no delay to Oxyrhynchus..."

(3) P.Fay.114,3ff.   100 A.D.
    εὖ οὖν πυήσας κομισάμενός μου τὴν ἐπιστολὴν πέμσις
    μυ Π.,...
    "On receipt of my letter you will kindly send
    my Pindarus,..."
(4) B.G.U.1676,11ff.   ii A.D.
    καλῶς οὖν ποιήσις λαβών μου τὰ γράμματα καὶ
    ἀναβῆνε τῇ προθεσμίᾳ τῆς κγ.
    "Be good enough then on receiving my letter to
    come up by the appointed date of the twenty-third."
(5) P.Oxy.1065,2ff.   iii A.D.
    λαβὼν τὰ γράμματα τοῦ υἱοῦ μου Θέωνος ἐξαυτῆς πάντα
    ὑπερθέμενος ἐλθέ μοι εἰς τὸ ἐποίκιον διὰ τὰ
    συμβάντα μοι.
    "On receipt of the letter of my son Theon put
    off everything and come at once to the homestead
    because of what has happened to me."

The extent to which these five examples include the three
formulaic elements may be set out in diagrammatic form.[34] The
letters are diagrammed in sequence.

	Item (1)	Item (2)	Item (3) (a)	(b)
(1)	ὡς ἂν λάβητε τ. ἐπιστολ.	παραγίνεσθε		...φέρε
(2)	ὡς ἂν ἀναγνῶτε τ. ἐπιστ.	...παραγέν.		
(3)	κομισάμενός μου τ. ἐπισ.	πέμσις		...πέμσις
(4)	λαβών μου τὰ γράμματα	ἀναβῆνε...	ἐὰν δὲ...	
(5)	λαβὼν τὰ γράμματα...	ἐλθέ...	ἐὰν δὲ...	

    b. Joy Expressions

    Koskenniemi suggests that expressions of joy in the non-
literary papyri are tied to the arrival of a letter. These
statements, he suggests, reveal two motifs: (a) relief over
the other's welfare; (b) the significance of the correspondence
for the writer.[35] Not all joy expressions are explicated by
these two motifs nor are they always found in the body-opening,
but a predominant percentage both relate to the reception of
the letter and open the body.

(1) P.Elephant.13,2f.   iii B.C.
    παραγενομένου Σανῶτος ἐκομισάμην τὴν παρὰ σοῦ
    ἐπιστολήν, ἣν ἀναγνοὺς ἐχάρην ἐπὶ τῶι με αἰσθέσθαι
    τὰ κατὰ σέ.
    "On the arrival of Sanos I received your letter,
    and it was a pleasure to read it and hear your
    news."

(2) P.Lond.42,7ff.   168 B.C.
κομισαμένη τὴν παρὰ σοῦ ἐπιστολὴν παρ' Ὥρου,...
ἐπὶ μὲν τῶι ἐρρῶσθαί σε εὐθέως τοῖς θεοῖς
εὐχαρίστουν,...
"When I received your letter from Horus, (in
which you announce that you are in detention
in the Serapeum at Memphis,) for the news that
you are well I straightway thanked the gods,..."

(3) P.Lond.43,3f.   ii B.C.
πυνθαναμένη μανθάνειν σε Αἰγύπτια γράμματα
συνεχάρην σοι καὶ ἐμαυτῆι...
"Having ascertained that you are learning the
Egyptian script, I rejoiced for you and for myself..."

(4) P.Mich.483,3ff.   Reign of
χάριν σοι ἔχω τῇ φιλανθρωπίᾳ περὶ τοῦ   Hadrian
ἐλαίου καθὼς ἔγραψέ μοι Πτολεμαῖος
παρειληφέναι αὐτό.
"I thank you for your kindness about the olive
oil, as Ptolemaeus wrote to me that he had received it."

(5) P.Giss.21,3f.   ii A.D.
λίαν ἐχάρην ἀκούσασα ὅτι ἔρρωσαι καὶ ἡ
ἀδελφή σου...
"I rejoiced exceedingly when I heard that both
you and your sister were well..."

(6) B.G.U.332,6f.   ii/iii A.D.
ἐχάρην κομισαμένη γράμματα, ὅτι καλῶς
διεσώθητε.
"I rejoiced when I received your letter, that
you are well."

c. Statements Signalling Previous Communication

        Reference to previous communication in the non-literary
papyri is as varied as that between individuals or families
today. There are stylistic devices, nonetheless, which commonly refer to past associations. We have already analyzed
two stereotyped means of referring to previous communication:
complaints about failure to write and περί with the genitive.
We may now analyze two additional conventions, in the body-
opening, referring to previous communication.

        i. *The Addressor's Reproach*
        The body is sometimes opened by means of the addressor's
reproach of the addressee (because the addressee has failed to
do something). The addressor complains, in such instances,
either that he should not need to write at all (ex.4) or that
he has already written too many times (exx. 1-3,5).

(1) P.Hib.44,1ff.   253/52 B.C.
ἐγράψαμέν σοι πρότερον περὶ τῶν...; ὁρῶντες
δέ σε καταραθυμοῦντα...
"I have written to you before concerning the...;
but seeing that you are negligent..."

(2) P.Mich.69,2ff.   240 B.C.
καλῶς ποιήσεις τὸ ἱερεῖον, περὶ οὗ σοι
πλεονάκις γέγραφα καὶ ἐνώπιον πλεονάκις
εἴρηκα,...
"Kindly order the pig concerning which I have
written several times and several times have
spoken in person..."

(3) P.Oxy.1061,2ff.   22 B.C.
ἐπειδὴι καὶ ἄλλοτέ σοι ἐγράψαμεν καὶ οὐ
διήτησαι ἡμᾶς καὶ Ἀ. τῶι ἀδελφῷ σου τὰ νῦν
ἀνάγκην ἔσχον παρακαλέσαι...
"Since I have written to you at other times and
you have not brought about an agreement between
us, and also to your brother Apollonios, I have
now been obliged..."

(4) P.Oxy.532,3ff.   ii A.D.
ἔδει μέν σε χωρὶς τοῦ με γεγραφέναι σοι διὰ
Σαήτου ἀναπέμψαι τὰς (δραχμὰς) κ, εἰδὼς ὅτι...
"You ought without my writing to you to have
sent me by Saëtas the twenty drachmae, for you
know that..."

(5) P.Tebt. 423,2ff.   iii A.D.
καὶ ἄλλοτέ σοι ἔγραψα ὑπομιμνήσκων περὶ τῶν
ἔργων καὶ ἔμαθον εἰληφότα παρ' Ἀματίου τὸν
ἄρακα.
"I have written to you on other occasions to
remind you about the work, and I have heard that
you have received the aracus from Amatius."

ii. *Compliance Statements*

The body of the letter is introduced in some letters by
reference to previous instruction. Either: (a) the addressor
recalls a previous instruction which he gave to the addressee
(cf. exx. 3 and 4 below), or (b) the addressor mentions the
instruction given to him by the addressee (exx. 1, 2, 5).[36]

(1) P.Cairo Zen.59426,3f.   260-250 B.C.
καθότι μοι ἔγραψας τὴν πᾶσαν ἐπιμέλειαν
ποιοῦμαι ὅπως ἂν μηθεὶς...
"in accordance with what you wrote to me I am
taking the utmost care that no one (troubles your
people)."

(2) P.Mich.54,1f.   248 B.C.
καθότι ἔγραψας, ἀπέδωκα Ἀρτεμιδώρωι...
"In accordance with what you wrote, I received
Artemidorus..."

(3) P.Mich.202,3ff.   105 A.D.
     ὡς ἠρώτηκά σε καταπλέουσα περὶ τοῦ παιδίου...
     "As I asked you when I was on the point of sailing
     down, regarding the child..."
(4) P.Warren.14,5ff.   ii A.D.
     καθὼς ἐνεθειλάμεθα τῇ ἀδελφῇ σου ῾Α. περὶ...
     οἴδαμεν ὅτι οὐκ ἀμελήσει...
     "As we instructed your sister Arsous concerning
     (the one hundred twenty drachmae), we know that
     she will not neglect..."
(5) P.S.I.1080,3f.   iii A.D.
     καθὼς ἐνετίλω Τααμοίτι περὶ οἰκήσεως ἵνα
     μεταβῶμεν, εὕραμεν...
     "In accordance with your instructions to Taamois
     about a house for us to move into, we found..."

2. *The Body-Closing*

     The transition from the middle of the body to the body-
closing, like the transition from letter-opening to body-opening, is a major transition. But the phraseology and the idea
(function) of the body-closing are even more stereotyped, perhaps, than the body-opening. The body-closing functions in
two discrete, though not necessarily separate, ways: (1) as
a means of finalizing the principal motivation for writing (by
accentuating or reiterating what was stated earlier in the
body); (2) as a means of forming a bridge to further communication.[37]
     Both these two functions of the body-closing, and the re-
lation of the body-closing to the remainder of the letter, may
be better comprehended, perhaps, by reference to an actual
letter.

letter-opening: ῾Αχιλλᾶς ῾Απολλωνίῳ τῷ πατρὶ χαίρειν.

body-opening: θαυμάζω πῶς τοισούτων ἀνελθόντων μετὰ
                   καὶ κτηνῶν κενῶν οὐκ ἔπεμψας Σαραπάμμωνα,
                   εἰδὼς ὅτι χρία αὐτοῦ ἐστὶν ἐνθάδε.

body-middle: μέχρι νῦν οὐδίς σε ἐπεζήτεσε. ὁ ἀναδούς
                   μοι τὸ ἐπιστόλιον ἀνέφαινε λέγων ὡς
                   ἐκπλέκη ῞Αρειος δοὺς τὰ κολλήματα τῷ
                   βασιλικῷ. οὐκ ἐπόησε αὐτὰ ἐπισταλῆναι.

body-closing: διὼ γράφω σοι ἵν᾽ εἴδῃς σὺ εἴ τι δέον
                   ἐστὶ τί πράξῃς, εἰδὼς ὅτι, εἰ μὴ σὺ
                   παραγένῃ, λύσιν οὐ λαγχάνι τοῦτο· διὼ
                   μὴ ἀμελήλῃς.

letter-closing: ἐρρῶσθαι εὔχομαι. (P.Mert. 80, ii A.D.)

letter-opening: "Achillas to his father Apollonius, greeting.

body-opening: I am surprised that, when so many have come up country, and that with beasts un-laden, you have not sent Sarapammon, for you know there is need of him here.

body-middle: Up to the present no one has inquired after you. The man who handed me the letter declared in so many words that Areius will get you out of it, having given the rolls to the royal scribe; he did not have them sent.

body-closing: So I am writing to you in order that you may know, if there is anything neces-sary, what you are to do; for you know that, if you are not present, this affair finds no solution. So do not neglect this."

letter-closing: I pray for your well-being.

The only letter-opening convention in the letter above is the salutation. Immediately following the salutation, the body is introduced by an expression of astonishment, employing the verb θαυμάζω.[38] The background item, explicating the occasion for the expression of astonishment, is stated subsequently, conveyed by the subordinate clause, the beginning of which is indicated by the participial form (v) of the disclosure formula (εἰδὼς ὅτι). The body-middle begins, presumably, immediately succeeding this background item, though no recognizable formula is employed. The body-closing, in turn, is signalled by the "motivation for writing" (iii) form of the disclosure formula, which reiterates the principal matter of information of the preceding body. Having reiterated the primary message of the body, the addressor concludes the body-closing with the respon-sibility phrase διὸ μὴ ἀμελήλης. The only letter-closing con-vention is the health-wish (ἐρρῶσθαι εὔχομαι), which immediately follows the responsibility phrase.

In this specific letter, the two principal functions of the body-closing are intertwined. The occasion for writing relays matters demanding the addressee's immediate action. The basis of future communication, concomitantly, depends on how (or *whether*) the addressee responds to the claims made in the motivation for writing formula.

Having sketched the general lineaments of the body-closing, we may now turn to the specific formulae which are employed to implement it.

I have been able to identify four common types of body-closing formulae. Two of these four formulaic types were previously analyzed as "general" transitional devices.[39] All four types will be analyzed, however, either because the specific form of the formula is distinct or because the same formula carries a different meaning in the body-closing. The total impression derived from the presentation of these formulae, it is hoped, will also provide a more distinct impression of the contours and nature of the body-closing.

   a. Disclosure Formulae

The body-closing commonly employs only one disclosure formula as noted in the analysis of general transitional devices, and it is the motivation for writing formula (iii). The function of this formula in the body-closing is roughly comparable to that of the fuller form in the body-opening; instead of calling attention to some information following, however, the addressor calls attention to the preceding information, or some aspect of the preceding information in the body.

(1) P.Mich.10,13f.   257 B.C.
     γέγραφα οὖν σοι ὅπως εἰδῆις.
     "I wrote to you, therefore, that you might
     know."
(2) P.Tebt.747,16f.   243 B.C.
     ἔγραψα οὖν σοι ἵνα εἰδῆις τὴν σαυτοῦ ἀμέλειαν.
     "I have written therefore to you in order that
     you may realize your own carelessness."
(3) P.Par.43(=U.P.Z.66),4   154 B.C.
     γέγραφ' ἱμεῖν ἵνα εἰδῆται.
     "I have written to let you know."
(4) P.Oxy.299,4f.   late i A.D.
     καὶ Διονυσίῳ προστάτῃ Νεμερῶν κέκρηκα (δραχμὰς)
     η καὶ ταύτας οὐκ ἔπεμψε, ἵνα εἰδῆς.
     "I have also lent eight drachmae to Dioysius,
     president of Nemerae, and he has not sent them
     back, this is to inform you."
(5) P.Mich.512,6   early iii A.D.
     διὸ γράφω σοι ἵν' εἰδῆς.
     "Wherefore I wrote you that you may know."
(6) P.Fay.129,8f.   iii A.D.
     ἵν' οὖν ἰδῆς ἀναφέρω σοι.
     "..., so I send this note to inform you."[40]

b. Expressions Urging Responsibility

The summons to responsibility, it was noted, may appear
elsewhere in the body but neither as often nor with such variety
of expression as in the body-closing. These phrases, like the
motivation for writing formula, call attention to previous material in the body. Their function is to urge the addressee to
be responsive regarding an earlier request.

Different formulae may be employed to implement these en-
treaties, depending on the nuance intended by the addressor.
Rather than list a number of examples it seems more profitable
to note different types of responsibility phrases and the intent commonly tied to each. Two of these phrases, employing
the verbs ἀμελέω and μέλω, were analyzed previously (7ff.,
exx.1-4,9-17) and are the responsibility phrases found throughout the body. They are most often employed to remind the addressee not to neglect something previously requested in the
body and often imply nothing regarding the harm or benefit that
will befall the addressee whether he be negligent or faithful.
The same phrases, however, occasionally hold threat or promise.

The other devices, the conditional clause and the phrase
μὴ ἄλλως ποιήσῃς "do not do otherwise",(exx. 5-8 on p.8), commonly imply a threat--whether explicit or veiled.[41] These responsibility statements are intended, if they are not heeded,
to endanger future relationship.

One remaining body-closing phrase may be discussed in connection with responsibility statements. The addressor occasionally urges the addressee to do something and then adds that the
addressee will grant him a favor by fulfilling the request.
Whereas threats are usually from the superior to the inferior
in the epistolary situation, these benefit phrases are between
equals or from an inferior to a superior. Since no examples
of this benefit phrase were presented previously, a few examples
are listed now, in order that the phraseology and function of
the phrase may be observed.

(1) P.Mich.6,4f.   257 B.C.
     ..., ἐπιστολὰς παρὰ τῶν φίλων λαβὲ πρὸς αὐτόν.
     τοῦτο δὲ ποιήσας εὐχαριστήσεις ἡμῖν;...
     "..., get letters of introduction to him from
     his friends. By doing so you will much oblige
     us.,,,[42]

(2) P.Grenf.II.14(c),7   iii B.C.
...χαρίεισαί μοι τοῦτο ποιήσας.
"...by doing so you will grant me a favor."
(3) P.Tebt.766,15ff.   136 B.C.
τοῦτο δὲ ποιήσας ἔσῃ μοι κεχαρισμένος.
"By so doing you will confer on me a kindness."
(4) P.Tebt.56,15ff.   late ii B.C.
τοῦτο δὲ πόησας ἔσῃ μοι κεχαρισμένος εἰς τὸν
ἅπαντα χρόνον.
"If you do this, you will oblige me for all time."

    c. Courtesy Request for a Letter

    Requests for a letter in the body-closing, unlike the body-
opening, are usually pleasant.[43] These requests usually have
the following form: γράφε δὲ καὶ σὺ ἡμῖν ὧν ἂν χρείαν ἔχῃις
("But write concerning whatever you have need"). This formula
follows a request(s), stated earlier in the body, and it functions as a courteous means of repaying the favor, which was
asked in the previous request.

(1) P.Hib.64,19ff.   264/63 B.C.
χρὴ δὲ καὶ γράφειν μοι περὶ ὧν ἂν χρείαν ἔχῃς.
"And you must write me about anything you require."
(2) P.Grenf.II.36,14f.   95 B.C.
περὶ ὧν ἐὰν αἱρῆτε γράψατέ μοι...
"Write to me about any matter that you choose..."
(3) P.Mich.483,5f.   reign Hadrian
καὶ σὺ δὲ περὶ ὧν ἐὰν χρείαν ἔχῃς γράφε μοι,...
"And you write me about anything you want,..."
(4) P.Brem.52,9ff.   ii A.D.
περὶ ὧν θέλεις, γράφε μοι ἥδιστα ποιήσοντι.
"Write to me for whatever you want, knowing
I will gladly do it."
(5) P.Oxy.1218,8f.   iii A.D.
περὶ οὗτινος αἰὰν χρῇζῃς ἡδέως ποιοῦντι
ἀνόκνως δήλωσον.
"Tell me freely about anything you want and I
will do it gladly."

    d. Notification of a Coming Visit

    The major function of the letter, according to Koskenniemi,
was to represent a form of "life-together" during a time of spa-
tial separation, i.e., to turn absence into presence, *apousia*
into *parousia*.[44] But the letter was something of a substitute,
at best, for the actual presence. The actual presence, whatever

the nature of that togetherness, carried greater force for the mutual relationship. It is not surprising, therefore, that we often find references to coming visits in the body-closing as the means whereby the relationship, already implicit in the epistolary situation, is empowered. The coming may be regarded, therefore, by the addressee--depending on the nature of the to-getherness--as neutral (e.g., ordinary business matters), bene-ficial, or threatening.[45]

Neutral

(1) P.Oxy.1757,22ff.   ii A.D.
κόμισαι παρὰ Θ. μάνια δύο καὶ τήρησόν μοι αὐτὰ ἕως ἀναβῶ, καὶ δήλωσόν μοι.
"Receive two vessels from Theon and hold them for me until I come, and then show them to me."

(2) P.Oxy.1666,15ff.   iii A.D.
θεῶν οὖν βουλομένων, πρὸς τὴν ἑορτὴν... πειράσομαι πρὸς ὑμᾶς γενέσθαι...
"If the gods will, I will therefore try to come to you for the feast..."

(3) P.Oxy.1763,9ff.   iii A.D.
λέγουσι δὲ ὅτι μέχρι ιε θέλομεν ἐξελθεῖν σὺν θεῷ.
"But they say that we hope to depart on the 15th., god willing." (A note from Sopartrus to his sister, explaining that his departure had been delayed, but that he hoped to start on the 15th.)

Beneficial

(4) P.Hib.66,4ff.   228/27 B.C.
ὡς δ' ἂν παραγένωμαι ἀπὸ τῆς...τοῦ χαλκοῦ συνλαλήσω σοι ὥστε σε μὴ διὰ κενῆς εὐχαριστῆσαι ἡμῖν.
"And so soon as I arrive from the delivery (?) of the copper I will have a conversation with you, so that you shall not oblige me to no pur-pose."

(5) P.Oxy.743,41f.   2 B.C.
καλῶς δὲ γέγονεν τὸ ταχὺ αὐτὸν ἐλθεῖν, ὑφηγήσεται γάρ σοι.
"It is well for him to come quickly, for he will instruct you."

(6) P.Oxy.1216,17ff.   ii/iii A.D.
καὶ νῦν δήλωσόν μοι περὶ ὧν χρίαν αἴχεται παρ' ἐμοί, θεῶν γὰρ θελόντων, σπεύδω ἐξορμῆσαι πρὸς ὑμᾶς.
"Tell me now about anything here you want, for with the help of the gods I am hastening to set out to you.

(7) P.Oxy.939,26ff.   iv A.D.
...παραμυθούμεθα δὲ αὐτὴν ἑκάστης ὥρας
ἐκδεχόμενοι τὴν σὴν ἄφιξιν.
"We comfort her by hourly expecting your arrival."

Threatening

(8) P.Tebt.759,9ff.   226 B.C.
διὸ καὶ σκόπει μήποτε ἀντὶ γνώσεως εἰς
διαφοράν σοι ἔρχωμαι.
"So take care that I do not come to quarrel with
you instead of being on good terms."

(9) P.Par.49(=U.P.Z.62),33ff.   ca 160 B.C.
εἰ δὲ δι' ἄλλο τι οὐκ ὀπτάνεταί μοι, γίνωσκε
σαφῶς ὅτι ἐὰν ἀναβῶ κἀγὼ προσκυνῆσαι, πρὸς σὲ
οὐ μὴ εἰσέλθω, εἰς δὲ τὰ Π. καταλύσω.
"But if he is keeping out of my sight for some
other reason, understand clearly that if I come
up to worship, I will not enter your door, but
will lodge with Protarchus."

(10) P.Oxy.113,27f.   ii A.D.
ὅτι ἔδωκας αὐτῶι δήλωσόν μοι ἵνα συνάρωμαι
αὐτῶι λόγον. ἐὰν δ' ἄρα μή, ἅμα τῷ υἱῶι μου
ἐξέρχομαι τοῦτο ἕνεκα.
"Let me know what you have given him that I may
settle accounts with him. Otherwise I and my son
will come for this purpose."

3. *The Body Middle*

The analysis of the body-middle, as suggested previously,
is difficult for a number of reasons.[46] The greatest analytical problem, perhaps, is the different value transitions may
have in the body-middle. Whereas the body-opening and the body-
closing are points of major transition, the body-middle may contain a number of transition points of unequal value. And,
whereas the idea (function) of the body-opening and the body-
closing is rather uniform (i.e., the opening lays the basis on
which the subsequent body unfolds, either by disclosing new
information or by alluding to previous communication, and the
closing rounds off the body by reiterating the motivation for
writing and by laying a basis for future communication), the
body-middle does not function at one level.

Definitions of the body-middle, therefore, will be rather
tenuous at best. And qualifications will be required at certain
points because of the variety found in the body-middle. Due
to the multiplicity of transitional devices and the inequality
of transitions, transitional constructions will be studied under

two headings: major transitional devices and minor (grammatical) devices. Examples from each of the categories cannot be cited, as was done previously. Only the transitional devices not investigated heretofore will be listed.

    a. Major Transitional Constructions

Formulaic

    i. *General*--We noted that four discrete formulae (disclosure formulae, reassurances, responsibility statements, and grief expressions) are employed in more than one part of the body. All four are employed in the body-middle.

    Four forms of the disclosure formula appear in the body-middle. Two of them, the fuller form (i) and the imperative (ii), occur infrequently, but usually make points of major transition.[47] The two remaining forms, the perfect indicative and participle, are more common, but usually perform a minor role.

    Two of the three remaining formulae, stereotyped grief expressions and responsibility statements, are more characteristic of another part of the body. Responsibility statements, for example, are more integrally connected with the body-closing. These statements, nonetheless, should be regarded ordinarily as major transitions in the body-middle because both their phraseology and their freighted meaning are indicative of major import. Stereotyped grief expressions, on the other hand, appear much more often in the body-opening. The paucity of such expressions in the body-middle is regarded as prohibitive by this author and no interpretation of their transitional value, therefore, will be suggested.[48]

    The percentage of reassurance expressions in the body-middle, in contrast to the two preceding formulae, is much higher than elsewhere in the body. Reassurances are characteristic of the body-middle and, with other characteristic constructions, lay a basis from which one may draw some conclusions regarding the nature and function of the body-middle.[49]

    ii. *Specific*--We now turn to the specific body-middle constructions, first to the formulaic transitions, and secondly to the non-formulaic devices that evidence affinity with the body-middle.

Two major types of formulae are commonly found in the body-middle: formulaic references to writing and set verbs of saying and informing. Stereotyped references to writing are of four types, two of which have a past orientation and two of which refer to the future. The following instances are illustrative.

Reference to the Past

(a)

(1) P.Cairo Zen.59060,10   257 B.C.
ἔγραψας δέ μοι θαυμάζεις εἰ μὴ κατέχω ὅτι τούτοις
πᾶσι τέλος ἀκολουθεῖ.
"You wrote me that you were surprised at my not
understanding that all these things are subject
to toll."

(2) B.G.U.846,9f.   ii A.D.
αἴγραψά σοι ὅτι γυμνός εἴμει.
"I wrote to you that I am naked."

(3) P.Mert.81,8   ii A.D.
ἔγραψάς μοι περὶ τοῦ...
"You wrote to me concerning the..."

(4) P.Oxy.1066,8f.   iii A.D.
ἔγραψάς μοι διὰ τῆς ἐπιστολῆς ὅτι...
"You wrote to me in the letter '. . .'
(ὅτι recitativum)50

(b)

(5) P.Mich.55,11f.   240 B.C.
ἔγραψα δέ σοι καὶ περὶ Ἑρμοκράτου πρότερον,
διὰ...
"I wrote to you once before about Hermokrates,
because..."

(6) P.Tebt.408,11ff.   d A.D.
ἔγραψα δὲ καὶ Λυσιμάχωι τῶι φιλτάτωι μου περὶ
τῶν αὐτῶν ὡς καὶ σοί.
"I have written to my beloved Lysimachus also,
as well as to you, about the same persons."

(7) P.Mert.83,10ff.   late ii A.D.
ἐποίησα δὲ καὶ τὸν υἱόν σου γράψαι σοι περὶ
ἐμοῦ, καὶ ὁμοίως πάλιν τὸν ἐριοπώλην γράψαι
σοι διὰ τῆς ἐπιστολῆς αὐτοῦ.
"I have made your son to write to you about me,
and likewise again got the wool-dealer to write
to you in his letter."

(8) P.Oxy.1842.6   vi A.D.
ἔγραψα δὲ καὶ τῷ κυρίῳ Παμουθίῳ περὶ τούτου.
"I wrote to the lord Pamouthius also about this."

Reference to the Future

(a)

(9) P.Mich.43,2f.   253 B.C.
καλῶς οὖν ποιήσεις γράψας ἡμῖν ἀπολογισμὸν περί
τε τοῦ σίτου...
"Be good enough then to write us a statement concerning the corn..."

34

(10) P.Oxy.294,12ff.   22 A.D.
εὖ οὖν ποιήσις γράψας μοι ἀντιφώνησιν περὶ τούτων
εἶνα καὶ ἐγὼ αὐτὸς ἐπιδῶ ἀναφόριον τῷ ἡγεμόνι.
"I shall therefore be obliged if you will write
me an answer on this matter in order that I may
myself present a petition to the praefect."
(11) P.Oxy.300,4ff.   late i A.D.
..., περὶ οὗ καλῶς ποιήσεις ἀυτιφωνήσασά μοι
ὅτι ἐκομίσου.
"..., concerning which please send me an answer
that you received it."

                              (b)

(12) P.Tebt.22,11f.   112 B.C.
γράψον ἡμῖν τίς ἀδικεῖ.
"Tell us who is at fault."
(13) P.Oxy.1757,19   ii A.D.
γράψον μοι ἐπιστολὴν διὰ...
"Write me a letter by..."
(14) P.Oxy.1671,19   iii A.D.
γράψον οὖν ἵνα...
"Write therefore in order that..."

References to the "past" act of writing may be explicated
as follows: Formulaic items in type (a) references are: (1)
the past tense of the verb γράφω; (2) the unemphatic form of
the personal pronoun, designating the recipient; (3) the
object of the correspondence, introduced by one of the following
constructions: περί with the genitive (exx.3,5-8), ὅτι (exx.
1-2), διά (which means "through" in such contexts and refers to
the means whereby the addressee receives the correspondence,
ex.4). These items may be illustrated by the following diagrammatic example:

        1   2   3
      αἴγραψά / σοι /ὅτι (γυμνός εἰμί),
      "I wrote / to you / that (I am naked)"

The formulaic reference to past acts of writing in (b)
are like those in (a) in all respects but one, the addition of
the compound conjunction, δὲ καί. The use of δὲ καί, italicized
in examples 5-8, is a stereotyped way of referring to a second
act of writing, e.g., in letter 6 the addressor states, not
only that he has written the addressee, but that he has *also*
written to Lysimachus (the "also" is made explicit by δὲ καί).
Both of the "future" writing expressions request that the
addressee write to the addressor. The primary difference between the two forms is the degree of politeness with which the
request is made. Whereas letters with type (a) employ the con-

vention καλῶς (or εὖ ποιήσεις ("please" or "be good enough,"
etc.) as a polite circumlocution for the imperative,[51] the
harsher form of the imperative is used in letters under (b).[52]
The imperative form, like the imperative form (ii) of the disclosure formula, is found primarily in business letters.

The second major category of specific formulae in the body-
middle is verbs of saying and informing. Though the verb meaning
"to inform" is employed as a convention with discrete features,
the verb of saying (λέγω) seems to be confined neither to set
phrases nor to a certain form of the verb.[53] Before illustrating
these two conventions, a brief description of the formulaic use
of δηλόω is in order. The regular formulaic items are three,
καὶ/ δήλωσόν/μοι ("And inform me"). The conjunction, καί, is
normally first; the verb δηλόω, in the aorist imperative mood,
second; and the unemphatic form of the personal pronoun, in
the dative case (μοι), last. Most examples appear during the
Roman and Byzantine periods, and the formula is employed either
to introduce a new subject in the body-middle or to develop a
major aspect of the preceding subject. The formula, in either
case, marks a point of major transition.

(a) inform

(1) P.Fay.122,14f.   *ca* 100 A.D.
     ..., καὶ δηλωσόν μοι πόσαι ἐξέβησαν ἵνα εἰδῶ.
     "..., and inform me how many artabae came out
     so that I may know."
(2) P.Mert.22,12f.   ii A.D.
     καὶ πότε ἀναπλεῖν μέλλετε δηλώσατέ μοι,...
     "And tell me when you are intending to sail up,..."
(3) P.Oxy.1677,10   iii A.D.
     καὶ περὶ τῶν πρώτων ἐντολικῶν δήλωσόν μοι.
     "Tell me too about the first orders."
(4) P.Tebt.420,28f.   iii A.D.
     ...,καὶ δήλωσόν μοι ἀναγκαίως περί μου τί
     ἔπραξας.
     "..., and be sure to tell me what you have done
     about me."

(b) saying

(5) P.Mich.103,8f.   iii B.C.
     ἔφη δὲ καὶ ὁ Μάρκων ἀπεσταλκέναι...
     "Marcon also said that he has sent..."
(6) P.Oxy.744,11f.   i B.C.
     εἴρηκας δὲ Ἀφροδισιᾶτι ὅτι...
     "You told Aphrodisias '. . .' " (ὅτι *recitativum*)

(7) P.Oxy.932,3f.   ii A.D.
     ἐρεῖ σοι δὲ ᾿Απολινάρις πῶς...
     "Apolinarius will tell you how..."
(8) P.Mert.83,16f.   late ii A.D.
     λέγει δὲ Θερμούθιον ὅτι ἔλεγέν μοι Λυσανίας,
     φέρε χαλκόν, ἵνα ἀπενέγκω αὐτῷ,...
     "Thermouthion says, 'Lysanias said to me. "Bring
     some money, so that I may take it to him" ', . . ."[54]

Non-formulaic

    iii. *Grammatical and Topical Transitions*--At least five
types of non-formulaic constructions are employed in the body-
middle: (1) receipt-transfer statements; (2) the vocative;
(3) περί with the genitive; (4) tandem conjunctions; and
(5) single conjunctions. The first three categories were
analyzed earlier.[55] The two latter categories, though also
found in the body-opening and the body-closing, are used more
extensively in the body-middle.

    The tandem conjunction δὲ καί demands special attention
since it seems especially characteristic of the body-middle.
It was examined previously in connection with formulaic references to writing (33, exx. 5-8) in the body-middle, and
in that context was a means of referring to a *second* act of
writing. Δὲ καί also refers to an additional item--either
signalling the introduction of a new subject matter or a new
tack in the development of the present subject--elsewhere in
the body-middle. The importance which this non-formulaic construction may assume, as a transitional construction in the
body-middle, is amply illustrated in the following letter.

         letter-opening: Δημοφῶν Πτολεμαίωι χαίρειν.
         body opening: ἀπόστειλον ἡμῖν ἐκ παντὸς τρόπου τὸν
                           αὐλητὴν Πετῶυν ἔχοντα τούς τε φρυγίους
                           αὐλοὺς καὶ τοὺς λοιπούς, καὶ ἐάν τι δέηι
                           ἀνηλῶσαι δός, παρὰ δὲ ἡμῶν κομιεῖ.
         body-middle: ἀπόστειλον δὲ καὶ Ζηνόβιον τὸν
                           μαλακὸν ἔχοντα τύμπανον καὶ κύμβαλα καὶ
                           κρόταλα, χρεία γάρ ἐστι ταῖς γυναιξὶν
                           πρὸς τὴν θυσίαν. ἐχέτω δὲ καὶ ἱματισμὸν
                           ὡς ἀστειότατον. κόμισαι δὲ καὶ τὸν ἐριφον
                           παρὰ ᾿Αριστίωνος καὶ πέμψον ἡμῖν. καὶ τὸ
                           σῶμα δὲ εἰ συνείληφας, παράδος αὐτὸ
                           Σεμφθεῖ, ὅπως αὐτὸ διακομίσηι ἡμῖν.
                           ἀπόστειλον δὲ ἡμῖν καὶ τυροὺς ὅσους ἂν
                           δύνηι καὶ κέραμον κενὸν καὶ λάχανα
                           παντοδαπὰ καὶ ἐὰν ὄψον τι ἔχηις.
         letter-closing: ἔρρωσο. (P.Hib.54, *ca.* 245. B.C.)

letter opening:	Demophon to Ptolemaeus greeting.
body-opening:	Send me by hook or crook the flute player Petous with both the Phrygian and the other flutes; and if any expenditure is necessary, pay and you shall recover from me.
body-middle:	Send me also Zenobius the effeminate dancer with a drum and cymbals and castanets, for the women want him for the sacrifice; and let him be dressed as finely as possible. Get the kid also from Aristion and send it to me. And if you have arrested the slave, hand him over to Semphtheleus to bring to me. Send me also as many cheeses as you can, empty jars, vegetables of all sorts, and any delicacies that you may have.
letter-closing:	Good-bye.

The letter-opening and the letter-closing of the above letter are nothing more than a salutation and farewell. Though no identifiable formula occurs, we may presume that the body-opening begins immediately after the salutation. The movement to a new subject, signalled by the first occurrence of δὲ καί (each δὲ καί is underlined), indicates the beginning of the body-middle. Four additional transitions, each employing δὲ καί, occur in the body-middle. And, since no recognizable body-closing convention appears, we may assume--at least formally--that the last δὲ καί transition leads directly to the letter-closing. Additional examples of this tandem conjunction are listed below.

(1) P.Mich.58,16ff.   248 B.C.
κατέστησα δὲ καὶ τὸν 'Ε. ἐπὶ Νικάνορα περὶ τούτων...
"I also brought Etearchas before Nikanor about
this matter..."
(2) Revillout, *Melanges*,p.295(=W.Chrest.10),12f. 130 B.C.
ἐπισκοποῦ δὲ καὶ τὰς ἀδελφὰς...
"Look after my sisters also..."
(3) P.Tebt.408,11ff.   3 A.D.
ἔγραψα δὲ καὶ Λυσιμάχῳ τῶι φιλτάτῳ μου περὶ τῶν
αὐτῶν ὡς καὶ σοί.
"I have written to my beloved Lysimachus also,
as well as to you, about the same persons."
(4) P.Oxy.1488,13ff.   ii A.D.
γενοῦ δὲ καὶ εἰς τὸ ἐργαστήριον καὶ μάθε...
"Go also to the workshop and find out..."

b. Minor Transitional Constructions

Five non-formulaic constructions, employed in the body-middle, were analyzed earlier. Only two of these constructions,

the vocative and receipt-transfer statements, could actually be
considered major transitional constructions. The three remaining constructions, περί with the genitive, tandem and single
conjunctions, tend to be employed for minor transitions. Three
formulae, the use of λέγω and two forms of the disclosure formula (the perfect indicative [iv] and the participial [v]), are
also employed primarily for minor transitions.

    c. Summary Comments on the Body-middle

    The body-middle is both more diverse and more complex in
function than the body-opening or the body-closing. "Diversity"
and "complexity" are a means of calling attention to two discrete
though related, aspects of the body-middle. "Diversity" is the
primary means of calling attention to the *number* of functions
(e.g., the body-middle may develop the subject introduced in
the opening; new material of equal import may be introduced;
new material lacking the importance of the first subject may
be introduced, etc.), whereas "complexity" refers to the com-
plex *pattern* of functions the body exhibits by virtue of its
middle position. The body-middle plays the dual role, for example, both of developing initial body-opening statements and
also of anticipating closing statements and--if skillfully
executed--welds the two parts together.

    We may now summarize the transitional import of the various
body-middle constructions. The following usually signal points
of major transition: (1) the fuller (i) and imperative (ii)
forms of the disclosure formula; (2) the use of the vocative
case;[56] (3) statements of reassurance;[57] (4) the formulaic
phrase employing the verb of informing; (5) writing formulae;
(6) receipt-transfer statements.

    Constructions which are sufficiently elastic to function
in the role of either major or minor transition in the body-
middle are: (1) verbs of saying; (2) the tandem conjunction
δὲ καί; (3) περί with the genitive.

    The following constructions usually mark points of minor
transition: (1) the perfect indicative (iv) and participial (v)
forms of the disclosure formula; (2) conditional clauses. And
the use of single conjunctions is restricted exclusively--unless
such conjunctions accompany a formulaic phrase or other construction of transitional import--to minor transitions.

C. Summation: The Body's Phraseology and Function

1. *The "Idea" of the Body*

The fundamental and practical need that created the impetus to letter writing was the need to converse with someone from whom the writer is separated. It was the desire to turn, as Koskenniemi phrases it, *apousia* into *parousia*. The two major aspects of this need were the desire to maintain personal contact and the need to impart information.[58] The tripartite letter form (opening, body, and closing) emerged as a surrogate for spoken conversation in order to perform this dual role of imparting information and maintaining contact. The opening and closing parts of the letter, for example, are the primary means for extending greetings (i.e., maintaining personal contact), whereas the body is the "message" part of the letter (i.e., the means for imparting information). The proportion of the letter occupied by opening and closing, on the one hand, or the body, on the other, is generally an index to the primary intent of any given instance of the private Greek letter.

Since we already have a rather clear conception of the form and purpose of the letter-opening and the letter-closing, I have sought only to deal with the letter-body in this investigation. And, since it seems warranted to assume that the body is the "message" part of the letter, I have attempted to interpret the phraseology and function of the body in this light. Taking this assumption as a point of departure, the following comments seem appropriate to the definition of the body.

The general function of the body is the imparting of information to someone at a distance and the role that the respective body parts play in the execution of this function may be stated as follows. The body-opening posits the basis of mutuality (i.e., whether disclosing new information; recalling previous communication of which both parties are cognizant; or reassuring the addressee about the present status of a business matter; the body-opening introduces the most pressing matter of mutual concern).[59] The body-middle--once the basis of common concern has been introduced--carries the message forward; either by developing its relevant details, introducing new and equally important matters of mutual concern, or by introducing new but less important matters. The role of the body-closing may be

grasped on the basis of the interaction of its two principal
functions: (1) the means whereby the principal motivation
for writing is finalized (either by accentuating or reiterating
what was previously stated); (2) the means of establishing the
basis of future communication. An interaction results, for
example, when the reiteration of the motivation for writing *is*
the basis for future communication, e.g., the addressor threatens
the addressee regarding some negligence and suggests that he
will fulfill the threat through an actual visit should the
addressee not comply. The nature of the relationship connoted
in the reiteration of this principal motivation for writing
(whether good or bad), therefore, often tends to function as
the basis that funds future communication.

2. *Criteria for Identifying and Ordering Transitions*

The two primary criteria employed for the identification
and differentiation of transitional constructions within the
body are "stereotyped phraseology" and "position". The body
usually has three discrete sections: body-opening; body-middle;
and body-closing. Both body-opening and body-closing are
points of major transition in the body and are easily identified
by means of their position within the letter.[60] These transitions from letter opening to the opening of the body and from
body-closing to the letter-closing may also be identified as
points of major transition by means of the formulaic phraseology
employed at such points.

The body-middle is something of a bridge between the body-
opening and body-closing and, consequently, both its position
and phraseology are more difficult to identify.[61]

3. *The "Phraseology" of the Body*

The "idea" of the letter-body is informed, as I suggested
previously, by the transitional formulae which are characteristic of each of its sections. We review at this point, therefore, the characteristic formulae of each body-section.

The body-opening is frequently introduced by the following
formulae: (1) the disclosure formula (fuller [i] and imperative [ii] forms); (2) stereotyped requests (for a letter [couched
in the form of a complaint regarding failure to write] and for

the addressee to visit); (3) joy expressions; (4) formulaic references to previous communication (the "compliance" formula and the "addressor's reproach" formula).

The body-closing employs the following: (1) the motivation for uniting (iii) form of the disclosure formula; (2) responsibility statements; (3) the polite request for a letter formula; (4) formulaic references to a coming visit; (5) conditional clauses employed formulaically as a threat.

The body-middle has, it will be recalled, various transitional levels. Major transitions of a formulaic nature are: (1) reassurances; (2) the stereotyped use of the verb δηλόω; (3) writing formulae. Major transitions of a non-formulaic nature are: (1) receipt-transfer statements; (2) the use of the vocative case. Transitional constructions that may be employed for either major or minor roles are primarily non-formulaic and include the following: (1) the perfect indicative (iv) and participial (v) forms of the disclosure formula; (2) verbs of saying; (3) the tandem conjunction δὲ καί; (4) περί with the genitive case.

CHAPTER TWO

BODY OF THE PAULINE LETTER: PHRASEOLOGY AND STRUCTURE

Introduction

The purpose of this chapter is the structural analysis of
the body of the Pauline letter. Before turning to the specific
investigation, we need to fit the study of the letter-body into
the total pattern of issues connected with the literary analysis
of the letter. And, in order to frame the study of the letter-
body in this manner, it will prove helpful, perhaps, to review
briefly the recent studies and the present status of the analysis of the Pauline letter.

The literary analysis of the Pauline letters (and the New
Testament letters in general) has lagged behind comparable
literary advances in the Synoptic Gospels and Acts. For, though
we have developed techniques appropriate to the study of the
Synoptics and Acts ("form criticism" and "style criticism,"
respectively), we have not developed a corresponding tool for
the letters. This state of affairs is due, in large part, to
the heritage bequeathed to us by Adolf Deissmann. For Deissmann
suggested that Paul, like the common letter writer of his day,
constructed his letters in terms of the spontaneity of his own
feelings. Thus, apart from such necessary epistolary conventions as salutation, thanksgiving (the *proskynema* formula in
the papyri), and closing, the letter form was determined by the
needs of the moment and the author's own whim.[1]

Deissmann's thesis has at least two major flaws. One is
his suggestion that the form of the letter (both that of the
common Greek letter, preserved in the non-literary papyri, and
the Pauline letters) is chaotic, necessarily, because such is
the natural concomitant of letter-writing. The other defect
is in the form of an over-simplification, namely, his proposal
that the common letter tradition is the literary genre to which
the Pauline letter belongs.[2] Though a number of subsequent
studies have been eroding his thesis, we have hesitated, by
and large, to make alternative proposals on the form of the
Pauline letter. The first real broadside, perhaps, was fired
only recently by Robert Funk, who gathered up the collective

force of these studies (in addition to his own literary endeavors
on the Pauline letter) in an attempt to bring the whole of the
letter form into view.[3] We shall find it helpful, due to the
nature of his study, therefore, to summarize his comments on the
present status of the investigation.

He suggests, by way of preliminary hypothesis, that we will
work with more liklihood of success if we combine the close analysis of form with style and sequence analysis. He proceeds, thereupon, to adduce the respective contributions which each of these
types of literary analysis has produced. Form critical studies,
for example, have enabled us to identify the following discrete
elements within the Pauline letter: paraenesis; opening thanksgiving; salutation and closing; and other traditional material
(e.g., hymns, kerygmatic formulae, confessions, doxologies, and
benedictions). Style criticism, for its part, has functioned
as a means of calling attention to Paul's affinity with various
traditions, as well as to his own distinctive use of language.
And sequence analysis (of those passages containing Paul's theological argument) suggests that even the body of the letter is
more tightly structured than Deissmann proposed. The combined
force of these diverse labors indicates, decisively, that Paul
was not the undisciplined letter-writer we thought. And this
state of affairs is indicative, simultaneously, according to
Funk, of the manner in which we should approach the study of
the letter as a whole. Consequently, he turns, on the basis of
information gained from the preceding types of analysis, to a
proposal regarding the form of the Pauline letter and its con-
stituent elements.

Paul Wendland's discussion of the form of the letter,[4] in
Funk's opinion, is still normative. The letter, according to
Wendland, is comprised of salutation (sender, addressee, greeting)
and opening thanksgiving at the beginning; doxology, greetings,
and benediction at the close. Martin Dibelius had identified,
in addition, paraenesis in Paul, confined largely to a section
immediately preceding closing items (and dependent on a nonepistolary tradition prior to Paul).[5] Paul Schubert,[6] followed
by James Robinson[7] and Jack Sanders,[8] has extended the formal
analysis of the opening thansgiving (more appropriately called
hodaya or *beracha,* according to Robinson), including the formula
which opens the body. Funk contends that we may proceed even

further, and speak in a preliminary way of the theological body. For style and sequence analyses have enabled us to identify tightly organized and skillfully framed theological arguments which customarily form the body of the letter. In addition to the formal opening, referred to above, these tightly organized theological arguments regularly evidence a close interrelation of theological and practical concerns. These arguments, in turn, are formally concluded, on occasion, by an eschatological climax, corresponding to the eschatological climax which concludes the opening thanksgiving. Paul turns, finally (usually immediately prior to the paraenetic section), to the question of his apostolic relation to the congregation (recently identified and designated apostolic *parousia* by Funk[9]). Since each of these elements within the body will be taken up in my own investigation, we may now turn to Funk's suggestions on the number and the usual order of the letter elements.

The Pauline letter form may be provisionally defined as consisting of the following structural elements: (1) salutation (sender, addressee, greeting); (2) thanksgiving; (3) body, composed of a formal opening, connective and transitional formulae, concluding "eschatological climax" and apostolic *parousia*; (4) paraenesis; (5) closing items (greetings, doxology, benediction).

The preceding sketch, dependent primarily on Funk's study, provides an appropriate frame for discussing the purpose of this investigation. We may assume, with some confidence, that all of the major elements of the Pauline letter are now identified. It is also warranted to assume, however, that a great deal of work remains, both on the meaning of the whole and on the further elucidation of each of the parts. I am of the opinion, for example, that we have not adequately delineated the body of the Pauline letter. Though we have established some criteria for the formal opening, and Funk has made a rather thorough analysis of the body-closing, we still do not know how the theological argument (=the "body-middle") is formally conceived. Various discriminating studies have been made on the structure and development of the theological argument within the individual letter, e.g., Rudolf Bultmann's analysis of Paul's defense of his apostolic ministry in II Cor. 2:14-6:10,[10] but we have not identified (at least with any precision) those larger formal aspects of

the theological argument which are common from letter to letter.
I shall attempt to deal with such issues, shortly, but first
we must look at the question of methodology.

Two methodological guidelines are employed, concomitantly,
as means of making the approach to the structure of the body of
the Pauline letter as objective as possible: (1) Information
gained from the analysis of the common Greek letter (regarding
the idea, form, and phraseology of the body) provides one means
of determining and analyzing corresponding features in the body
of the Pauline letter. (2) The body of Philemon, Romans, and
Galatians, is analyzed as the first step within the Pauline
corpus, since their integrity, apart from Romans 16, is generally assumed. On the basis of data gleaned from the two preceding steps, the following may be identified as body sections:
Philem.8-22; Gal. 1:6-5:12; Rom. 1:13-11:36 and 15:14-33; Phil.
1:12-2:30; 4:10-20; I Thess. 2:1-3:13; I Cor. 1:10-4:21; and
II Cor. 1:8-7:16.

I must acknowledge, before proceeding further, that the
two preceding guidelines do not permit us to interpret all the
material within the body of the Pauline letter, i.e., there are
constituents within the body (e.g., traditional material such
as hymns, kerygmatic formulae, etc.) which are not derived from
either the common letter tradition or from Paul's own creativity.
On the other hand, by comparing the transitional phraseology
of the Pauline letter with the corresponding phraseology of the
private Greek letter, and by observing formal similarities from
letter to letter, so that we learn the substructure of the Pauline
letter-body, we will be enabled to suggest, perhaps, how Paul
used his sources.

The preliminary identification of the structural units within each of the body sections, and the transitional phraseology
whereby the borders of such units are established, will be set
out in the analysis of Philemon, Galatians, and Romans, subject,
of course, to correction, should subsequent analysis of the four
remaining letters necessitate modification.

A. Analysis of Philemon, Galatians, and Romans

1. *Preliminary Sketch of Structure and Phraseology*

We noted, in the analysis of the private Greek letter,
that the body of the letter commonly has three discrete sections

("body-opening," "body-middle," and "body-closing"), which may be identified both by position within the body, and by the characteristic phraseology within each section. The point at which each of these three body-sections is introduced, for example, is a point of major transition, which may often be identified by the phraseology employed.[11] The same three body divisions may be identified, and by the same or similar phraseology, in the three Pauline letters under consideration.

The principal difference between the body of the Pauline letter and that of the private Greek letter is length. All three divisions of the body are more extensive in Paul than in the papyri. And this fact alone makes us wary of assuming simple congruence; we may anticipate that Paul will have modified the common letter tradition at various points with respect to transitional phraseology, just as he has modified the letter tradition with respect to length.

This difference in length may lead us to assume, in addition, the possibility (perhaps the necessity?) of additional divisions or subdivisions in the Pauline letter-body. Two of the three letters, Galatians and Romans, contain evidence of numerous divisions and subdivisions. We find an introductory statement regarding the occasion for writing in the body-opening of both Galatians and Romans. This initial statement (or statements) is followed by a tightly framed and skillfully drawn theological argument, which, though introduced in the body-opening, receives its actual impetus and characteristic nuance in the first statement of the body-middle and extends into the body-middle. This theological section is followed by another discrete section (extending to the end of the body-middle), less artistically drawn and more akin to the *diatribe* in style, where the "principle" espoused in the preceding section is applied more concretely to Paul's readers.[12] This section, in turn, is followed by a body-closing section, initiated by a statement briefly recapitulating the message of the body (i.e., the occasion for writing), in which Paul demands that the claims advocated earlier be accepted. He enforces his apostolic authority at this point by three discrete means, which are woven integrally into a tripartite structure.

We find, therefore, that the segment of the body previously and neutrally defined "body-middle" is comprised of two discrete and major parts in Paul. In addition, the section called "body-closing" in Paul may be divided further into three tightly inter woven parts. We observe, finally, that the body-opening section of the body is considerably longer and employs more body-opening formulae than is characteristic of the papyri.

The characteristic phraseology, the nature of additional subdivisions, and the precise limits of each section of the Pauline letter-body will be analyzed sequentially under the following headings: body-opening; body-middle; and body-closing.

2. *Body-Opening in Philemon, Galatians, and Romans*

We may provisionally identify the following body-opening sections: Philem. 8-14; Gal. 1:6-14; and Rom. 1:13-15.[13] Six different body-opening formulae appear within these three sections. We take up these formulae separately and in connection with individual letters, beginning with Philemon.

a. Philemon

An expression of joy is commonly employed in the private Greek letter as a means of opening the body of the letter. Koskenniemi suggested, it may be recalled, that expressions of joy are tied to the arrival of a letter and reveal two motifs: (1) relief over the other's welfare; (2) the significance of the correspondence for the writer. The reception of news-- whether by letter or another type of report--is presupposed also in Philem. 7 as the basis of Paul's joy.[14] But, whereas the joy expression may be a veiled request for further correspondence in the papyri, the occasion for Paul's joy (Philemon's ability to refresh the saints) provides the basis (a "background") from which Paul makes an explicit and material request that similar refreshing be extended to himself.[15] A request, then, is the second body-opening formula in Philemon. But the two formulae are complementary and, consequently, should be regarded as a single unit. The request proper, i.e., excluding the background, may be cited in full:

Διό, πολλὴν ἐν χριστῷ παρρησίαν ἔχων ἐπιτάσσειν σοι τὸ ἀνῆκον, διὰ τὴν ἀγάπην μᾶλλον παρακαλῶ τοιοῦτος ὢν ὡς Παῦλο πρεσβύτης, νυνὶ δὲ καὶ δέσμιος Χριστοῦ Ἰησοῦ, παρακαλῶ σε περὶ τοῦ ἐμοῦ τέκνου, ὃν ἐγέννησα ἐν τοῖς δεσμοῖς, Ὀνήσιμον τόν ποτέ σοι ἄχρηστον νυνὶ δὲ καὶ σοὶ καὶ ἐμοὶ εὔχρηστον, ὃ ἀνέπεμψά σοι, αὐτόν, τοῦτ᾽ ἔστιν τὰ ἐμὰ σπλάγχνα ὃν ἐγὼ

ἐβουλόμην πρὸς ἐμαυτὸν κατέχειν, ἵνα ὑπὲρ σοῦ μοι διακονῇ
ἐν τοῖς δεσμοῖς τοῦ εὐαγγελίου, χωρὶς δὲ τῆς σῆς γνώμης
οὐδὲν ἠθέλησα ποιῆσαι, ἵνα μὴ ὡς κατὰ ἀνάγκην τὸ ἀγαθόν
σου ᾖ ἀλλὰ κατὰ ἑκούσιον.

"Accordingly, though I am bold enough in Christ to command
you to do what is required, yet for love's sake I prefer
to appeal to you--I, Paul, an ambassador and now a prisoner
also for Christ Jesus--I appeal to you for my child, Onesimus, whose father I have become in my imprisonment. (Former-
ly he was useless to you, but now he is indeed useful to
you and to me.) I am sending him back to you, sending my
very heart. I would have been glad to keep him with me,
in order that he might serve me on your behalf during my
imprisonment for the gospel; but I preferred to do nothing
without your consent in order that your goodness might not
be by compulsion but of your own free will."

Formal items within the request (i.e., introduction of the request period with the conjunction διό, the statement of request
with the verb παρακαλῶ, and the content of the request introduced
by περί) correspond roughly to such requests found in the papyri.[16]
The principal difference between this request and the common type
found in the private Greek letter, however, is the extensive
length of the former. We ought also to call attention to the
more oblique and reticent nature of the request.[17]

A request and its background (i.e., the occasion or basis
from which the request is asked), therefore, form the body-opening segment of Philemon: a section extending from Philem. 7-14
and comprising roughly half of the total body.

b. Galatians

Paul's letter to the Galatians, like Philemon, has a considerably longer body-opening section than that commonly found
in the papyri letters. The section, which extends from 1:6-14,
contains four different body-opening formulae. The disclosure
formula in 1:11f. is the keystone in the body-opening around
which the other three formulae build. Both the introductory
formula (the expression of astonishment in 1:6) and the second
formula (the statement of compliance in 1:9) function as background items to the introduction of the message of the body in
1:11.

The expression of astonishment in 1:6f., the formula introducing the body-opening, may be cited in full:

Θαυμάζω ὅτι οὕτως ταχέως μετατίθεσθε ἀπὸ τοῦ καλέσαντος
ὑμᾶς ἐν χάριτι Χριστοῦ εἰς ἕτερον εὐαγγέλιον, ὃ οὐκ ἔστιν

50

ἄλλο εἰ μή τινές εἰσιν οἱ ταράσσοντες ὑμᾶς καὶ θέλοντες μεταστρέψαι τὸ εὐαγγέλιον τοῦ Χριστοῦ.

"I am astonished that you are so quickly deserting him who called you in the grace of Christ and turning to a different gospel--not that there is another gospel, but there are some who trouble you and want to pervert the gospel of Christ."

The expression of astonishment in the opening is one of the principal means in the papyri whereby the addressor reproaches the addressee's failure to write.[18] This expression, in turn, functions as the background of the request for a letter. The expression of astonishment in Galatians, like the common Greek letter, is both an expression of extreme dissatisfaction and an intimation that communication has broken down, but it does not function as the background of a request for a letter. The object of Paul's dissatisfaction is not the Galatians' failure to write but their apparent rejection of the gospel with which he had previously evangelized them.

The second body-opening convention in Galatians, the statement of compliance in 1:9, takes the following form:

ὡς προειρήκαμεν, καὶ ἄρτι πάλιν λέγω, εἴ τις ὑμᾶς εὐαγγελίζεται παρ᾿ ὃ παρελάβετε, ἀνάθεμα ἔστω.

"As we have said before, so now I say again, if any one is preaching to you a gospel contrary to that which you received, let him be accursed."

The body of the private Greek letter is sometimes opened by reference to previous instruction. Either: (1) the addressor reminds the addressee of instructions which he had been given and which are still not obeyed; or (2) the addressor informs the addressee that he has "complied" with his instruction.[19] The first form of the convention is employed in Gal. 1:9. Paul reminds the Galatians of instructions he had given them on a former occasion but instructions, on the basis of 1:6ff., which had not been obeyed.[20] The astonishment evidenced in 1:6 is intensified, therefore, by the fact that Paul had previously and explicitly warned the Galatians to guard against subversive propaganda.

The third and most important of the body-opening formulae in Galatians is the disclosure formula in 1:11f.:

γνωρίζω γὰρ ὑμῖν, ἀδελφοί, τὸ εὐαγγέλιον τὸ εὐαγγελισθὲν ὑπ᾿ ἐμοῦ ὅτι οὐκ ἔστιν κατὰ ἄνθρωπον·οὐδὲ γὰρ ἐγὼ παρὰ ἀνθρώπου παρέλαβον αὐτὸ οὔτε ἐδιδάχθην, ἀλλὰ δι᾿ ἀποκαλύψεως Ἰησοῦ Χριστοῦ.

"For I would have you know, brethren, that the gospel
which was preached by me is not man's gospel. For I did
not receive it from man, nor was I taught it, but it came
through a revelation of Jesus Christ."

The fuller form (i) of the disclosure formula in the papyri
commonly has the following form: γινώσκειν σε θέλω ὅτι. . .
("I want you to know that. . ."). Though this form of the disclosure formula is found in other parts of the body, it is predominant in the body-opening. This form of the formula, especially when the vocative is included, is predominantly a body-
opening formula in Paul also. Only three examples of the fuller
form with the vocative are found in Philemon, Galatians, and
Romans, and two of these are in the body-opening.[21] In both
instances, as in the papyri, these formulae signal the motivation for writing. We may anticipate further elaboration of
the subject matter disclosed in these passages, therefore, since
they signal the theme (or purpose) of the letter.

The "information" in Galatians is Paul's disclosure that
the gospel which he had preached to the Galatians is both of
divine origin and divine in nature. The earlier astonishment
that the Galatians had turned from this gospel (1:6f.), heightened by the fact that Paul had expressly instructed them to be-
ware of subverters (1:9), is the "background" which necessitates
a disclosure regarding the nature of the gospel preached to the
Galatians.

The fourth and final body-opening formula in Galatians is
the use of the verb ἀκούω in 1:13f.:

Ἠκούσατε γὰρ τὴν ἐμὴν ἀναστροφήν ποτε ἐν τῷ Ἰουδαϊσμῷ,
ὅτι καθ' ὑπερβολὴν ἐδίωκον τὴν ἐκκλησίαν τοῦ θεοῦ καὶ
ἐπόρθουν αὐτήν, καὶ προέκοπτον ἐν τῷ Ἰουδαϊσμῷ ὑπὲρ
πολλοὺς συνηλικιώτας ἐν τῷ γένει μου, περισσοτέρως
ζηλωτὴς ὑπάρχων τῶν πατρικῶν μου παραδόσεων.

"For you have heard of my former life in Judaism, how
I persecuted the church of God violently and tried to
destroy it; and I advanced in Judaism beyond many of
my own age among my people, so extremely zealous was I
for the traditions of my fathers."

It is not unusual to find ἀκούω in the body-opening since it is
a conventional word in the private Greek letter by means of
which the addressor introduces some report as the basis from
which the letter proceeds. Two irregularities are present in
Galatians 1:13f.; the report is not stated in the first person
and the object of the report is tied neither to an expression

of grief nor to a statement of anxiety.[22] The report Paul recounts is one which the Galatians already know--reinforcing the God-given character of his gospel. This formula then, like those in 1:6f. and 1:9, is a background item to Paul's thematic statement and occasion for writing given in 1:11f. On the other hand, both because of order and meaning, the formula leads away from the motivation for writing expressed in 1:11f. and represents a development of that statement. It has been suggested, for example, that the two criticisms leveled at Paul in 1:10-12 (i.e., that his gospel is κατὰ ἄνθρωπον in 1:10f. and that it stems παρὰ ἀνθρώπου in 1:12) are refuted in chiastic pattern, i.e., in reverse order: παρὰ ἀνθρώπου (1:13-2:21), κατὰ ἄνθρωπον (3:1-6:10).[23] The report in 1:13f., on this basis, marks the first item in the demonstration that the gospel, when it came to Paul, was not of human origin. But there are formal reasons, nonetheless, for contending that the body-middle, the beginning of which may be identified by the first major transition to the development of the body-opening theme, does not begin until 1:15.[24] I see no inherent reason, however, why the formula may not perform both roles, lending greater weight to the occasion for writing and also functioning as transition to a later and stronger statement which formally opens the body-middle.

c. Romans

The letter to the Romans, though considerably longer than either Philemon or Galatians, has a shorter body-opening section and only one identifiable formula, the polite form of the disclosure formula in 1:13:

> οὐ θέλω δὲ ὑμᾶς ἀγνοεῖν, ἀδελφοί, ὅτι πολλάκις προεθέμην ἐλθεῖν πρὸς ὑμᾶς, καὶ ἐκωλύθην ἄχρι τοῦ δεῦρο, ἵνα τινὰ καρπὸν σχῶ καὶ ἐν ὑμῖν καθὼς καὶ ἐν τοῖς λοιποῖς ἔθνεσιν.

> "I want you to know, brethren, that I have often intended to come to you (but thus far have been prevented), in order that I may reap some harvest among you as well as among the rest of the Gentiles."

Both the inclusion of the vocative as a formulaic item and the use of the disclosure formula as a means of stating Paul's motivation for writing, are points of similarity between this passage and the disclosure formula in Gal. 1:11f. A few of the formal items in 1:13 (notably the verb ἀγνοέω and the peculiar use of the double negative), however, make this example slightly different.[25]

The ostensible occasion for writing to the Romans is the disclosure of Paul's desire to visit, a desire stated earlier in the thanksgiving (1:10-12) and later concretized in the form of a promise to visit (15:14-33).

Brief amplification of the reason for the desire to visit is stated in 1:14f., immediately preceding the formal opening of the body-middle in 1:16. Were it not for this statement, one would have difficulty connecting the motivation for writing in 1:13 with the body-middle of 1:16ff., a situation much different than that in Philemon or Galatians, where the purpose for writing is extended and logically developed in the body-middle. And even the connection between 1:14f. and 1:16 is more dependent on catchword association--the use of the cognate words εὐαγγελίσασθαι in 1:15 and εὐαγγέλιον in 1:16--than on material continuity. The significance of this apparent lack of continuity will be taken up subsequently.

3. *Body-Middle in Philemon, Galatians and Romans*

a. Introduction and Procedure

We shall investigate the following passages in connection with the body-middle: Philem. 15-18; Gal. 1:15-4:31; and Rom. 1:16-11:36. Before we can turn to the text, however, we must deal with a number of preliminary factors which complicate this stage of the analysis and necessitate a different type of analytical procedure than that followed in the body-opening.

We were able to employ the body-opening conventions of the common letter tradition in the analysis of the body-opening of Philemon, Galatians, and Romans as a methodological guideline for the identification of major points of transition and as an index to the interpretation of specific formulae. This procedure cannot be employed in the study of the body-middle, however, owing to a lack of continuity between the papyri and Paul, particularly where the use of the major body-middle formulae are concerned.[26] The only convention Paul regularly employs to indicate a major body-middle transition, like the papyri, is the vocative.[27] Our primary data, consequently, must be derived from the Pauline letters themselves.

Internal features of the Pauline body-middle itself also complicate the analysis and frustrate the possibility of util-

izing the comparative method, so fruitful for the body-opening.
These three letters, leaving the question of formulaic similarities with private Greek letters aside, submit to only limited
comparison with each other. The length of the body-middle of
Philemon constitutes an additional problem: its brevity, corresponding more closely to the papyri, both prohibits meaningful
comparison and necessitates an analysis different than that followed subsequently in Galatians and Romans.[28] In what manner,
then, can we proceed with the investigation of the Pauline body-
middle? Certain aspects of the body-middle in Galatians and
Romans suggest a possible course.

It was observed earlier that the body-middle of both Galatians and Romans appears to fall into two large and discrete
parts.[29] The first part, immediately following the body-opening, is a tightly organized theological argument; the second
part, immediately following and extending to the close of the
body-middle, is constructed less tightly and is the place where
the principles espoused in Part I are further concretized in
light of the readers' situation. The structure is analogous,
therefore, but the implementation of the form varies.

Paul consistently employs a few constructions in a formulaic manner and at major points of transition. But these constructions are, by and large, tied to an individual letter and
confined to Part I of the body. It may be proposed, in consequence, that Paul has created transitional constructions which
are expressive of, and integrally interwoven into, the theological argument of the body.[30] These transitional constructions,
consequently, vary of necessity in Galatians and Romans, although
the same principle is at work in both, i.e., the use of constructions which are integrally tied to the theological argument.
With these factors in mind, we may now plot a course through the
body-middle of Galatians and Romans, taking Galatians as our
point of departure.

b.   The Body-Middle of Galatians

i.   *Part I*--The first segment of the body-middle extends
from 1:15-2:21. This segment of the body-middle coincides with
Paul's attempt to refute the charge that his gospel stems παρὰ
ἀνθρώπου. We can easily grasp the importance, therefore, of

the sequence of events related to Paul's commission as an apostle to the Gentiles.[31] Paul contends that his commission came from God considerably prior to any appreciable contact with the Christian leaders (the "twelve" or the "pillars") who could have bestowed a "derivative" authority upon him. Though refutation of the charge that his gospel is of human origin begins in 1:13f., it receives its characteristic flavor and first explicit formulaltion in the body-middle statement of 1:15-17:

Ὅτε δὲ εὐδόκησεν ὁ ἀφορίσας με ἐκ κοιλίας μητρός μου καὶ καλέσας διὰ τῆς χάριτος αὐτοῦ ἀποκαλύψαι τὸν υἱὸν αὐτοῦ ἐν ἐμοί, ἵνα εὐαγγελίζωμαι αὐτὸν ἐν τοῖς ἔθνεσιν, εὐθέως οὐ προσανεθέμην σαρκὶ καὶ αἵματι, οὐδὲ ἀνῆλθον εἰς Ἱεροσόλυμα πρὸς τοὺς πρὸ ἐμοῦ ἀποστόλους, ἀλλὰ ἀπῆλθον εἰς Ἀραβίαν, καὶ πάλιν ὑπέστρεψα εἰς Δαμασκόν.

"But when he who had set me apart before I was born, and had called me through his grace, was pleased to reveal his Son to me, in order that I might preach him among the Gentiles, I did not confer with flesh and blood, nor did I go up to Jerusalem to those who were apostles before me, but I went away into Arabia; and again I returned to Damascus."

The content alone of the above statement leads one to attribute pivotal importance to it. Formal items are also suggestive, however, of its import. The temporal clause, introduced by ὅτε δέ, carries a freighted meaning both here and at another crucial point within the theological argument (2:11ff.). The major transitional significance of this construction, twice used, is suggested by the fact that over three-fourths of Part I of the body-middle is dependent on the minor temporal clauses governed by these constructions. We may outline the sequence and rank:

1:15-2:10 Ὅτε δὲ εὐδόκησεν...
           Ἔπειτα... ἀνῆλθεν...
           ἔπειτα ἦλθον...
           Ἔπειτα ... ἀνέβην...

2:11-14:   Ὅτε δὲ ἦλθεν Κηφᾶς...
           πρὸ τοῦ γὰρ ἐλθεῖν...
           ὅτε δὲ ἦλθον...
           ἀλλ' ὅτε εἶδον...

The concluding segment of Part I (2:15ff.), which has three or four minor points of transition, is both less discursive and more argumentative and rhetorical. It may be taken both as the conclusion of Part I and possibly, becuase of stylistic features akin to the subsequent body-middle, as the transition to Part II.

ii. *Part II*--We may identify 3:1-4:11 and 4:21-31 in connection with this segment of the body-middle.[32] This segment,
in turn, may be roughly divided into three sections on the basis
of its major transitional constructions: 3:1ff.; 3:19ff.; and
4:28ff.[33] The distribution of the seven formulae within these
sections may be set out according to sequence and division:

(A) 1. Ὦ ἀνόητοι Γαλάται, τίς ὑμᾶς ἐβάσκανεν, οἷς κατ᾽
ὀφθαλμοὺς ᾽Ιησοῦς Χριστὸς προεγράφη ἐσταυρωμένος;

"O foolish Galatians! Who has bewitched you, before whose eyes Jesus Christ was publicly por-
trayed as crucified?" (3:1)

2. τοῦτο μόνον θέλω μαθεῖν ἀφ᾽ ὑμῶν ἐξ ἔργων νόμου
τὸ πνεῦμα ἐλάβετε ἢ ἐξ ἀκοῆς πίστεως;

"let me ask you only this: Did you receive the
Spirit by works of the law, or by hearing with
faith?" (3:2)

3. γινώσκετε ἄρα ὅτι οἱ ἐκ πίστεως, οὗτοι υἱοί εἰσιν
᾽Αβραάμ.

"So you see that it is men of faith who are the
sons of Abraham." (3:7)

(B) 4. Τί οὖν ὁ νόμος;

"Why then the law?" (3:19)

5. οὕτως καὶ ἡμεῖς, ὅτε ἦμεν νήπιοι, ὑπὸ τὰ στοιχεῖα
τοῦ κόσμου ἤμεθα δεδουλωμένοι· ὅτε δὲ ἦλθεν τὸ
πλήρωμα τοῦ χρόνου, ἐξαπέστειλεν ὁ θεὸς τὸν υἱὸν
αὐτοῦ, ... ἵνα τὴν υἱοθεσίαν ἀπολάβωμεν.

"So with us; when we were children, we were slaves
to the elemental spirits of the universe. But
when the time had fully come, God sent forth his
son, ..., to redeem those who were under the law,
so that we might receive adoption as sons." (4:3-5

(C) 6. ὑμεῖς δέ, ἀδελφοί, κατὰ ᾽Ισαὰκ ἐπαγγελίας τέκνα
ἐστέ.

"Now you, brethren, like Isaac, are children of
promise." (4:28)

7. διό, ἀδελφοί, οὐκ ἐσμὲν παιδίσκης τέκνα ἀλλὰ τῆς
ἐλευθέρας.

"So, brethren, we are not children of the slave
but of the free woman." (4:31)[34]

c. The Body-Middle of Romans

i. *Part I*--Unlike Galatians, there seems to be little
correlation in Romans between Paul's ostensible occasion for
writing, stated in the body-opening, and the subsequent body-
middle. The theme upon which at least Part I of the body-middle
builds is stated not in the body-opening but at 1:16-18, the

opening statement in the body-middle. Like Galatians, however, the body-middle is built around a chiastic pattern which, in this instance, is dependent on the statement that opens the body-middle. And, on the basis of the elements stated in this theme, we may propose that Part I includes 1:16-4:25. This statement should be cited in its entirety, therefore, since it provides the themes around which the larger divisions of Part I revolve.

οὐ γὰρ ἐπαισχύνομαι τὸ εὐαγγέλιον· δύναμις γὰρ θεοῦ ἐστιν εἰς σωτηρίαν παντὶ τῷ πιστεύοντι,'Ιουδαίῳ τε πρῶτον καὶ "Ελληνι. δικαιοσύνη γὰρ θεοῦ ἐν αὐτῷ ἀποκαλύπτεται ἐκ πίστεως εἰς πίστιν, καθὼς γέγραπται· ὁ δὲ δίκαιος ἐκ πίστεως ζήσεται.
    'Αποκαλύπτεται γὰρ ὀργὴ θεοῦ ἀπ' οὐρανοῦ ἐπὶ πᾶσαν ἀσέβειαν καὶ ἀδικίαν ἀνθρώπων τῶν τὴν ἀλήθειαν ἐν ἀδικίᾳ κατεχόντων, . . .

"For I am not ashamed of the gospel: it is the power of God for salvation to every one who has faith, to the Jew first and also to the Greek. For in it the righteousness of God is revealed through faith for faith; as it is writ-ten, 'He who through faith is righteous shall live.'
    For the wrath of God is revealed from heaven against all ungodliness and wickedness of men who by their wicked-ness suppress the truth."

The gospel of which Paul is not ashamed in 1:16 is defined in terms of itw two principal attributes (Power and Righteous-ness) in 1:17f. The latter attribute, righteousness, is further delineated on the basis of its two manifestations, justifying righteousness (which may be designated Δικαιοσύνη[1] because of its initial sequence) and condemning righteousness (ὀργή, desig-nated Δικαιοσύνη[2] because of initial sequence). These two attributes are taken up in reverse order: condemning righteous-ness (ὀργή, 1:18-2:12), justifying righteousness (Δικαιοσύνη[1], 2:13-3:22), and power (Δύναμις, 3:22-4:25). The limits of each of these sections may be defined not only in terms of content but also on the basis of the distinctive constructions at each of the major points of transition. The major transitional de-vice in Part I, as in Galatians, is itself expressive of the nature of the theological argument and, consequently, is tight-ly woven into the fabric. The formulaic construction in this case is οὐ γάρ (first stated in 1:16) and it marks the major junctures in Part I. The structure of Part I may be best pre-sented, perhaps, by abstracting the principal body-middle formu-lae in proper sequence and division.

1:16-2:12:	οὐ γὰρ ἐπαισχύνομαι τὸ εὐαγγέλιον.
	οὐ γὰρ ἐστιν προσωπολημψία παρὰ τῷ θεῷ.
2:13-3:22:	οὐ γὰρ οἱ ἀκροαταὶ νόμου δίκαιοι παρὰ τῷ
	θεῷ, ἀλλ' οἱ ποιηταὶ νόμου δικαιωθήσονται.
	οὐ γὰρ ὁ ἐν τῷ φανερῷ 'Ιουδαῖός ἐστιν,...
	Τί οὖν τὸ περισσὸν τοῦ 'Ιουδαίου,...;
	Τί οὖν;
	οὐ γάρ ἐστιν διαστολή
3:22-4:25:	οὐ γάρ ἐστιν διαστολή·
	οὐ γὰρ διὰ νόμου ἡ ἐπαγγελία...
	Οὐκ ἐγράφη δὲ δι' αὐτὸν μόνον...,ἀλλὰ καὶ δι'
	...τ. πιστεύουσιν ἐπὶ τὸν ἐγείραντα 'Ιησοῦν
	τὸν κύριον ἡμῶν ἐκ νεκρῶν, ...

It may be observed that οὐ γάρ introduces and closes each section but the last.[35] The theological force of this transitional
construction may be explicated by reference to an underlying
definition of the gospel which is threaded throughout the argument: the gospel is divine, *not* human.

　　ii. *Part II*--Romans 5:1-11:36, the applicatory segment of
the body-middle, divides into two large sections: 5:1-8:39 and
9:1-11:36. Two hypothetical auditors within Part I (1:16-4:25),
"spiritual Israel" and "Israel according to the flesh," are
taken up separately in connection with their relation to the
gospel: true Israel (5:1-8:39), Israel according to the flesh
(9:1-11:36).

　　Neither section appears to open with a distinctive transitional construction.[36] Their limits may be established, nonetheless, by other formal means. The closing of Part I (4:13-25)
for example, establishes the opening limits of the earlier section of Part II at 5:1ff. And a kind of eschatological conclusion to the section is begun in 8:18 and formally concluded in
8:38f. (Paul's affirmation of confidence in God's ability to
consummate the eschaton). The conclusion of this section in
turn sets the opening limits of the second section of Part II
at 9:1ff. The closing of the latter division is signalled by
an exclamation in 11:33 which concludes as an outburst of praise
in vs. 36.[37] Other major points of transition within the two
sections may be taken up together since the same conventions
are employed throughout. Though it is at times questionable
whether they are so consistently employed, as is οὐ γάρ in
Part I, to signal major shifts, three discrete constructions
are employed: οὐ γάρ, ἄρα οὖν, and τί οὖν.[38]

The questionable relation of the body-opening to the body-
middle in Romans, an issue which arose earlier, may now be taken
up. The more practical part of the body-middle (Part II, 5:1-
11:36) does not appear to reflect the specific connection with
the Roman congregation that we might expect. This state of affairs goes with the preceding observation that the ostensible
occasion for writing stated in the body-opening, i.e., the desire to visit, is not developed within the body-middle. We
could expect, on the basis of both the papyri and Galatians,
some continuity between these two segments of the body. How
can we explain, then, the failure either to elaborate on the
desire to visit or the lack of personal references (even in the
most applicative segment) in the body? John Knox has probably
provided the most satisfactory solution in his suggestion that
Rom. 1:1-15:13 may have been constructed by Paul as a general
letter which could be particularized as occasion demanded.[39]
This explanation fits well, both with internal structural features outlined heretofore and with additional features of the
body-closing to be taken up subsequently.

4. *Body-Closing in Philemon, Galatians and Romans*

   a. Introduction and Procedure

   The primary function of the body of the common Greek letter, it was suggested in Chapter One, was the imparting of information to someone separated by distance. And, whereas the
body-opening plays the role of "disclosing" a pressing matter
of mutual concern, the body-closing commonly functions both as
the means of finalizing the motivation for writing (either by
reiterating or accentuating what was stated earlier) and as the
bridge to future correspondence.[40] The theological body-closing in Paul (i.e., Philem., Gal., Rom.) has a similar function
and evidences some similarity in phraseology with the private
Greek letter.

   The theological body-closing in Paul, at least in respect
to inclusion of the same formal items, is more stereotyped than
either the body-opening or body-middle. Both because of internal similarity, therefore, and on account of points of resemblance with nonliterary papyri letters, the analysis of the
body-closing is greatly facilitated. Three discrete formulaic

units are found in the body-closing and, because passages em-
bodying each of these formulae are similar (in function if not
phraseology) from letter to letter, letters may be compared at
each of the formulaic sections.

Philem. 19-22, Gal. 5:1-12, and Rom. 15:14-33 comprise
these three body-closing units, which may be divided according
to the following terminology and sequence: (1) the motivation
for writing-responsibility formula (in which Paul briefly reiterates the message of the body and urges appropriate response to
it); (2) the confidence formula (by which Paul affirms confidence in an appropriate response from his readers); (3) implementation of the apostolic *parousia* formula (through which Paul
expresses his intention or hope to pay a personal visit). These
formulae, illustrated in proper sequence on the following page
in Table 1, will be analyzed in turn.

This section of the body which I have defined neutrally
"body-closing" is analyzed also by Robert Funk, who suggests
that the separate aspects of Paul's role as apostle converge
in this discrete section and may be appropriately designated,
therefore, "apostolic *parousia*."[41] His nomenclature derives
from the internal evidence of the body-closing itself. Paul
appears to regard his apostolic "presence" to the congregations
under three different but related aspects: the aspect of the
letter, the apostolic emissary, and his own personal presence.

The worth both of Funk's analysis and the value of conclusions drawn subsequently from this study may be better fo-
cused by comparing the two studies. The comparison here can
only be anticipatory, and detailed analysis will be reserved
until the individual formulae are taken up. The first two formulaic categories (motivation for writing-responsibility formula and confidence formula) could be subsumed under Funk's former category, "the aspect of the letter," and the third formula
(implementation of the apostolic *parousia*) corresponds to his
latter category, "Paul's own personal presence." The second
aspect of Paul's apostolic presence suggested by Funk, "the
apostolic emissary," does not come into consideration at this
point, since not one of the present three letters contains
the item.

Funk employs Rom. 15:14-33, the most elaborate and formally
structured of passages having to do with the apostolic *parousia,*

TABLE I—STRUCTURAL UNITS IN THE APOSTOLIC *PAROUSIA* OF PHILEMON, GALATIANS, AND ROMANS

Motivation for Writing-Responsibility Formula

Philem.19	ἔγραψα...	ἐγὼ Παῦλος	ἐγὼ ἀποτίσω·ἵνα μὴ λέγω...σεαυτόν μοι προσοφείλεις.
Gal.5:2	λέγω...	Ἴδε ἐγὼ Παῦλος	ὅτι ἐὰν περιτέμ. Χ. ὑμᾶς οὐδὲν ὠφελήσει.
Rom.15:14	ἔγραψα..	..καὶ αὐτὸς ἐγὼ..	ὡς ἐπαναμιμ. ...διὰ τ.χάριν τ. δοθεῖσάν μοι...εἰς τὰ ἔθνη
15:15		.τολμηροτέρως δὲ	

Confidence Formula

Philem.21	πεποιθὼς	ἐγὼ	τῇ ὑπακοῇ σου...	εἰδὼς ὅτι καὶ ὑπὲρ ὃ λέγω ποιήσεις.
Gal.5:10	πέποιθα		εἰς ὑμᾶς ἐν κυρίῳ	ὅτι οὐδὲν ἄλλο φρον.·ὁ δὲ ταράσ. ὑμᾶς...
Rom.15:14	Πέπεισμαι	αὐτὸς ἐγὼ	...περὶ ὑμῶν,	ὅτι καὶ αὐτοὶ μεστοί ἐστε ἀγαθωσύνης,...
15:15				

Implementation of the Apostolic Parousia

Rom. 15:14-33

1a	14-15a	4a	30ff.
2	15b-21	4b	32
3c	22	5a	32b; cf.24d
3a	23b		
3b	24b		
3d	24c		
3f	28b		

Rom. 1:8ff.

4a	10b
4b	10b
3a	11a;cf.15
5a-b	11b-12
3b	13a
3c	13b
5b	13c

Philem. 21f.

[5a]	20b]a
1a	21
3f	22a
3b	22b
4a	22b

Gal. 4:12-20

3b	20a
5b(?)	20b

a[ ] indicates that the theme in question does not occur in the Apostolic *parousia* proper, but in proximity to it (The limits of the Apostolic *parousia* are those suggested by Funk, "The Apostolic *Parousia*: Form and Significance," 253f. I extend the limits of the Apostolic *Parousia* in Philemon to include 19-22 and add Gal. 5:2-12 as a discrete apostolic *parousia* section. Both additions are discussed in the subsequent analysis of the text.)

as a model of its individual items and order. After making minor modifications of the rubrics established in Romans by appealing to parallel passages, he submits the following item
analysis and order in tabular form:

"(1) γράφω (ἔγραψα) ὑμῖν ..., stating Paul's (1a) disposition (participle) or (1b) purpose (ἵνα-clause) in writing.
     (2) The basis of Paul's apostolic relation to the recip-
ients.[42]
     (3) Implementation of the apostolic *parousia*.
         (3a)   Desire, eagerness to see (come to) them
         (ἐπιποθέω, σπουδάζω and cognates).
         (3b)   Hope (ἐλπίζω), wish (θέλω), intention
         (προτίθεμαι) to see (come to) them.
         (3c)   Hindrance to his coming (ἐνκόπτω, κωλύω),
         or delay.
         (3d)   'To be sent on by you' (προπέμπω).
         (3e)   Dispatch of an emissary, which takes the form
         (a) ἔπεμψα ὑμῖν (name); (b) ὅς (credentials); ἵνα
         (or infinitive: purpose).
         (3f)   Apostolic *parousia*, which takes the form of
         an announcement or promise of a visit, or that a
         visit is expected, hoped or prayed for(cf. 3b, 4a).
     (4) Invocation of divine approval and support for the
apostolic *parousia*.
         (4a)   The Prayer for his presence may be a request
         for prayer, their prayer, his own prayer.
         (4b)   The convention, 'if God wills.'
     (5) Benefit from the apostolic *parousia* accruing
         (5a)   to Paul,
         (5b)   to the recipients,
         (5a-b) to the two mutually."[44]

Employing this construct as a point of departure for the whole
body-closing, we may now take up in turn the three formulaic
categories, posited by this author, in relation to the construct.

     b.   The Motivation for Writing-Responsibility Formula

     The purpose of the body-closing of the private Greek
letter, after the information introduced in the body-opening
has been carried forward in the body-middle (either by the development of its relevant details or by the introduction of new
information), is to repeat the occasion for writing and to lay
the basis for future correspondence.

     These two functions are reflected in the four principal
body-closing formulae.[45] The motivation for writing formula
which introduces the body-opening (γέγραφα οὖν σοι ἵνα εἰδῇς,
"I wrote to you in order that you might know"), by repeating

the reason for writing, performs the first of these two body-
closing functions. This formula may finalize the message of
the body, if the addressor desires only to disclose information.
On the other hand, if the addressor expects some response to
the imparted information, one or more of the three remaining
body-closing formulae may be employed subsequently. When the
addressor expects a response, he employs, most often, one of
the "responsibility" phrases. These phrases, depending on the
particular one employed, may promise benefit, be relatively
neutral, or be threatening.

The implementation of the body-closing in these three
Pauline letters parallels, roughly, what we find in the papyri.
Though the form (the "phraseology") is not identical, the intent and sequence of the formulae are similar. The body-closing
is introduced uniformly, for example, by a surrogate motivation
for writing formula. I say "surrogate" because, though the
formula does employ the verb meaning "to write," γράφω, as in
the papyri, Paul does not actually state the convention in the
form of a disclosure (i.e., he does not use the verb "to know,"
γινώσκω). In addition, the function of the summons to responsibility (the "responsibility" phrase) is not stated separately
in Paul, but is implicit in his motivation for writing statement.
The construction may be appropriately designated, therefore, the
motivation for writing-responsibility formula.

The motivation for writing-responsibility formula divides
into three formal items, which are set out in Table 1 on
page 61. The appropriate passages may be repeated here in
diagrammatic form.

	(1)	(2)	(3)
Philem. 19	ἐγὼ Παῦλος	/ ἔγραψα...,/	ἐγὼ ἀποτίσω· ἵνα μὴ...
Gal. 5:2	Ἴδε ἐγὼ Παῦλος /	λέγω... /	ὅτι...
Rom. 15:14f.	καὶ αὐτὸς ἐγὼ /	ἔγραψα... /	ὡς...

The three formal items within the formula are: (1) a formulaic
statement of authorship (especially ἐγὼ Παῦλος); (2) reference
to the act of writing (ἔγραψα);[46] and (3) reiteration of the
reason for writing (introduced by various means: ἵνα-clause,
ὅτι, ὡς). The first item in this formula, the statement of
authorship, is an oblique means by which Paul asserts his apostolic authority and, consequently, the claim to an appropriate
response (=the "responsibility" phrase); a claim which, if un-
heeded, seems to hide the barbs of threat just below the surface.[47]

c. The Confidence Formula

The greatest formal difference between the body-closing in
Paul and the corresponding section in the common letter tradi-
tion is Paul's use of a "confidence" formula, a formula which
has no parallel in the papyri. The role of this formula in the
Pauline body-closing may be explicated in relation to its order.
And, for the sake of comparison, we may diagram, in order, the
fullest form of the body-closing in Paul and in the private
Greek letter.

	the papyri		*Paul*
(1)	motivation for writing	(i)	motivation for writing-responsibility phrase
(2)	responsibility phrase	(ii)	confidence formula
(3)	anticipated visit	(iii)	anticipated visit

The confidence formula is Paul's means of alleging confidence
in the fulfillment of the claims set forth in the preceding motivation for writing-responsibility formula. The formula has
four formal items (cf. Table 1 on page 61), which may be set
out, once again, in diagrammatic form.

	(1)	(2)	(3)	(4)
Philem. 21		/ πεποιθὼς	/ τῇ ὑποκοῇ σου	/ εἰδὼς ὅτι
Gal. 5:10	ἐγὼ	/ πέποιθα/εἰς ὑμᾶς ἐν κυρίῳ		/ ὅτι...
Rom. 15:14f.	ἐγὼ	/ Πέπεισμαι	/ περὶ ὑμῶν	/ ὅτι...

These items may be identified thus: (1) the emphatic use of
the pronoun (ἐγώ); (2) the perfect form of the verb πείθω,
by which Paul alleges his "confidence;" (3) the specification
of the basis of confidence, defined as residing either in the
Lord (Gal. 5:10) or in Paul's addressees (Philem. 21 and Rom.
15:14); and (4) explicit mention of the object concerning which
Paul is confident (introduced by ὅτι).

Though the confidence clause may be a way of softening the
claims stated earlier in the motivation for writing formula, it
is more feasible that the clause is a genuine assertion of confidence. The key to understanding the convention, perhaps, is
the qualification ἐν κυρίῳ in Gal. 5:10. Just as Paul can make
legitimate demands on his congregations because he has a divine
commission, so also can he expect that the divine message which
he proclaims will effectively run its course. Paul's confidence,

it seems, is vested in the eschatological power of the gospel
itself.[48]

   d. Comparison with Item 1 of Robert Funk's Construct

   Item 1 (stating either Paul's [1a] disposition or [1b]
purpose in writing) of Robert Funk's construct, on the preceding
analysis of the first two body-closing formulae, is subject to
correction. His (ia) and (ib) roughly correspond, though in
reverse order, to the motivation for writing-responsibility
formula (i.e., =1b) and the confidence formula (i.e., =1a).
Differences emerge, however, in the identification of formal
items, the question of relevant passages, and the precise function of each formula.[49]

   In regard to Paul's purpose in writing, Funk identifies
neither the formal items nor the passages which I equate with
the motivation for writing formula.[50] He accounts for the in-
significance of the first body-closing formula both in terms
of the sequence of the body-closing formulae, and because of
Paul's explicit statement concerning the significance which
he attached to his personal presence (=apostolic *parousia*).[51]
I agree with the suggestion that the characteristic trajectory
is from 1 through 3e, i.e., from the weaker (the motivation
for writing formula) to the stronger medium (the formulaic apostolic *parousia* section), but I would contend on *formal* grounds
that the first body-opening formula (=item 1 in Funk's construct)
plays a role in the total schema as important as that of Paul's
intention to visit.[52] It is important, in addition, to be able
to determine on formal grounds where the body-closing begins
and the motivation for writing formula--especially the words
ἐγὼ Παῦλος ἔγραψα--enables us to identify the formal opening of
the apostolic *parousia*.

   Minor corrections may also be adduced in connection with
Funk's identification of Paul's disposition in writing (ia).
In addition to the question of order, i.e., the formula actually occupies second, not first, position, we may note that the
key term in the formula is the perfect form of the verb πείθω.

   e. Implementation of the Apostolic *Parousia* Formula

   The addressor's desire or promise to visit,[53] is usually
the last element in the body-closing of the private Greek letter.

The reference to a coming visit may be either separate from or related to the other body-closing formulae. If the formula is related, however, the anticipated visit carries either a nuance of threat or benefit. The visit should be construed, in either case, as the means of empowering the relationship already latent in the correspondence.

The body-closing is concluded, similarly, in the Pauline letters by Paul's reference to an anticipated visit--either that of himself or that of an apostolic emissary. And, once again like the common letter tradition, the nature of the visit may be determined largely on the basis of the tenor of the preceding elements in the body-closing.

This third formulaic unit within the body-closing corresponds to the third aspect, according to Funk, under which Paul regarded his apostolic presence to his congregations, his own presence. Due to the extensive length and lack of consistent order of items within the final formulaic body-closing unit, Funk's symbols for these (and their order) are employed in Table I on page 61. I concede both to the number and sequence of items suggested by Funk at this point. The only additional contribution which I make, in fact, is the suggestion that Gal. 5:11f. should be added to his list. This alone, however, is of some import.

In Philem. 22 and Rom. 15:22-23 Paul states his intention to pay his addressees a visit. The anticipated visit, in both passages, succeeds the two body-closing formulae (the motivation for writing-responsibility formula and the confidence phrase) described above. We anticipate, on the analogy of Philemon and Romans, that the announcement of a visit will follow the same two formulae in Galatians, but no intention to visit is stated. It is passing strange that the primary medium by which Paul makes his apostolic authority effective is not present in Galatians. How may we account for this conspicuous absence?

Funk suggests that the letter itself is underscored as the bearer of Paul's apostolicity in Galatians--Gal. 4:12-20 and 6:11 functioning structurally in a way comparable to the apostolic *parousia* in the other letters--because neither the dispatch of an emissary (3e) nor his own presence (3f) were possible.[54] But, in any event, in his opinion, Paul does not call attention to the letter itself at the customary place. I agree both with

his explanation of the absence of (3e) and (3f) and with his
suggestion that 4:12-20 and 6:11 are possible substitutes for
the apostolic *parousia*. I take issue, however, with his suggestion that Paul fails to include an apostolic *parousia* section
at the proper point.

Two discrete body-closing formulae have already been identified, in my analysis, at the proper point in the body, i.e.,
(1) the motivation for writing-responsibility formula in 5:2ff.
(cf. analysis on 62f.), and (2) the confidence formula in 5:10
(analysis on 64f.). And, since neither (3e) nor (3f) are present here (for reasons already adduced), may we not expect a
surrogate for the intention to visit in this same context? There
are legitimate bases for identifying Gal. 5:11f. precisely in
this way.[55] The passage, for purposes of demonstration, may be
cited in full:

> Ἐγὼ δέ, ἀδελφοί, εἰ περιτομὴν ἔτι κηρύσσω, τί ἔτι
> διώκομαι; ἄρα κατήργηται τὸ σκάνδαλον τοῦ σταυροῦ.
> Ὄφελον καὶ ἀποκόψονται οἱ ἀναστατοῦντες ὑμᾶς.

> "But if I, brethren, still preach circumcision, why
> am I still persecuted? In that case the stumbling-
> block of the cross has been removed. I wish those
> who unsettle you would mutilate themselves!"

Could it be that for the sake of the gospel Paul has been taken
prisoner? On this basis, or a similar extenuating circumstance,
5:11a ("But if I, brethren, still preach circumcision, why am
I still persecuted?") could be interpreted as a repudiation of
those who question his authority, i.e., he cannot visit the
Galatians precisely because his proclamation of the gospel as
an apostle has made him captive to circumstances beyond his con-
trol.[56] And on this basis perhaps we may better understand the
real force of the wish in 5:12: "I wish those who unsettle you
would mutilate themselves!" The confidence "in the Lord,"
voiced in 5:10, concerns not only the restoration of the Galatians but also the condemnation of those who have misled the
Galatians. Is it not conceivable, on this basis, that the curse
of 5:12 should be construed as the execution, albeit absent in
the body, of Paul's apostolic authority? If this interpretation
is correct, the force of Paul's authority in the written word
comes to the fore here as at no other point in the Pauline corpus. But, even if this latter interpretation is too forceful,
there are material reasons for insisting that 5:11f. should be

construed both as the surrogate for Paul's own apostolic presence
and as an explanation of his inability to be present.

B. I Thessalonians, Philippians, I & II Corinthians

1. *Introduction and Procedure*

The following elements and sequence--on the basis of previous work on the form of the Pauline letter[58] and in the light
of observations suggested in this study--may be proposed as a
working hypothesis for the structure of the Pauline letter: (1)
salutation (sender, addressee, greeting); (2) thanksgiving; (3)
body, with a formal opening, theological argument (which has
both a more theoretical [Part I] and a practical [Part II] part)
and closing (=apostolic *parousia*); (4) paraenesis; (5) closing
items (greetings, doxology, benediction).

The three letters already examined conform, with slight
deviation, to this form.[59] A greater amount of liberty seems
to be initially evidenced, however, in the implementation of
this form in the present group of Pauline letters. One innovation concerns the expanded form of one element within two of
the letters to the apparent exclusion of another of the elements.
In addition to this kind of innovation, we may call attention
to what probably constitutes an additional element within the
body section of the letter. This element, which has been identified and named ("the eschatological climax") by Robert Funk,
immediately precedes the apostolic *parousia* section in I Thess.
2:13-16, Phil. 2:14-18, and I Cor. 4:1-13.[61]

Neither of the preceding innovations, however, are so dam-
aging--at least to the analysis of the theological body--that
the four letters must be analyzed separately or that they cannot
be investigated in relation to the theoretical form of the body
derived from the analysis of Philemon, Galatians, and Romans.
With regard to the latter of the innovations, the form of the
body will be corrected where necessary to include the eschatological period, i.e., immediately following Part II of the body-
middle and immediately preceding the apostolic *parousia*. With
regard to the former innovation, I have found that each of these
letters maintains some degree of functional continuity with the
usual elements and order and, therefore, all four of the letters
may be fruitfully subjected to comparison.

I Thessalonians, Philippians, I and II Corinthians will be
taken up and analyzed, consequently, both in relation to each
other and according to the following tripartite division of the
body: (1) body opening; (2) body-middle, with the addition of
the eschatological climax period when applicable; (3) body-
closing (apostolic *parousia*).

2. *Body-Opening*

Despite peculiarities elsewhere in the body, the body-opening of these four letters affords evidence of a more consistent
pattern from letter to letter than that found in Philemon, Galatians, and Romans. Only three different formulae (disclosure
formula, joy expression, request formula) are employed in these
letters--compared with *six* in Philemon, Galatians, and Romans--
and the disclosure formula is found in three of the total five
references (I Thess. 2:1; Phil. 1:12, II Cor. 1:8. The request
formula appears in I Cor. 1:10 and the opening joy expression
in Phil. 4:10).

In order to present a clearer picture of the different
types of body-opening formulae and the number of times each
occurs in the seven letters of this investigation, we may summarize the formulae in descending order, according to the number
of times each appears:

> (1) disclosure formula (Gal. 1:11; Rom. 1:13; I Thess. 2:1;
> Phil. 1:12; II Cor. 1:8)
> (2) request formula (Philem. 8ff.; I Cor. 1:10)
> (3) joy expression (Philem. 7; Phil. 4:10)
> (4) expression of astonishment (Gal. 1:6)
> (5) statement of compliance (Gal. 1:9)
> (6) formulaic use of ἀκούω (Gal. 1:13f.)

Apart from Galatians, three body-opening formulae are employed
in these letters. Two of these three formulae, the request
formula and the joy expression, occur only twice, whereas the
remaining formula, the disclosure formula, is found five times.
Paul apparently preferred to use the disclosure formula to open
the body and it may be suggested that--unless the epistolary
situation itself warranted--he probably used the formula when-
ever possible.

On the basis of the preceding observations, it is hoped
that we are better prepared to read the body-opening segments
of the present four letters. The following may be tentatively

identified: I Thess. 2:1-4; Phil. 1:12-18; 4:10-13(?); I Cor.
1:10-16; II Cor. 1:8-12. They shall be taken up for analysis,
apart from Phil. 4:10ff., in the order in which they are listed.

a. I Thessalonians

The body-opening of the very first letter may constitute a
problem in analysis because Paul Schubert suggests that I Thessalonians has no "main body." He contends that the thanksgiving
itself--which, he suggests, extends from 1:2-3:13--constitutes
the main body of I Thessalonians, since it contains all the primary information Paul wished to convey.[62] This letter may be
an example, in other words, of one of the two types of innovations earlier suggested in connection with this group of Pauline
letters, namely, the expanded form of one element in the letter
(the "thanksgiving" here) to the exclusion of one of the other
elements (the "body" here). I endorse, heartily, both Schubert's
suggestion that the thanksgiving has a singularly important
epistolary function[63] and that I Thessalonians does not have a
"body" of doctrinal or practical information like Paul's letters
customarily have. I propose, nonetheless, that the body *is* a
structural element--though, to be sure, taken up into, shaped
by, and logically dependent on, the thanksgiving.

In order to proceed from this point, it is necessary briefly to demonstrate that we have a "body" in I Thessalonians. We
may reiterate the formal elements of the body adduced from the
study of Galatians and Romans at the start, and then we may turn
to the question of the corresponding elements in I Thessalonians.
The formal elements of the body are:

> (i) a formal body-opening, in which the occasion for
> writing is set forth;
> (ii) the body-middle (=the theological argument proper
> in which the object of disclosure introduced in the
> body-opening is developed), with a more theoretical
> (Part I) and an applicative (Part II) part;
> (iii) the body-closing (=the apostolic *parousia*).

With regard to the body-opening in I Thessalonians, we note
that a major transitional construction (the disclosure formula),
though slightly irregular in form, is found at the appropriate
point in the letter (2:1f.).[64] This formula and a subsequent
background item extend through 2:4.

The motivation for writing disclosed by this formula is
followed in 2:5 by another formula of major import. The latter
formula, because it--analogous to the corresponding section in
Galatians and Romans--is a construction expressly created by
Paul for this letter and a formula interwoven into the fabric
of the theological body, is probably the opening statement in
the body-middle. It gives nuance to the section which extends
through 2:12 (the end of Part I of the body-middle).

Part II of the body-middle, the applicative segment in
which the theological motifs of Part I are spelled out in relation to Paul's addressees, is introduced in 2:13 and extends
through 2:16. Due to the peculiar nature of the epistolary
situation, this segment at first appears to bear little resemblance to the corresponding portions of Galatians and Romans.
Note, for example, that the section is begun by the repetition
of the basic thanksgiving formula. The thanksgiving in this
particular instance, however, *is* an appropriate expression, in
retrospect, of the application of Paul's message to his addressees! Whereas Part I of the body-middle is the recollection of
the claims which emerged in the preaching of the gospel at
Thessalonica, Part II is a means of positing the evidence, retro-
actively, which demonstrates that the Thessalonians have been
able to *concretize* these claims in their own lives. Paul's
paean of thanksgiving is the appropriate means, therefore, for
introducing the applicative part of the body-middle.

The body-closing section of the body, also at the proper
point, extends from 2:17-3:10. This section corresponds structurally item for item with the three body-closing formulae identified in Philemon, Galatians, and Romans.

We find one additional element in the body of the letter,
however, the eschatalogical climax in 3:11-13. The presence
of this element is integrally bound up with the peculiar nature
of the letter. Functionally speaking, the thanksgiving itself
is the occasion for and message of the letter and, in accordance
with the general pattern evidenced elsewhere in the Pauline letters, the eschatological climax concludes the thanksgiving section.

On the basis of these preliminary observations, peculiarities of expression notwithstanding, the body section of I Thessalonians matches the proposed structure point for point and in

the proper order.[65] We may now turn to a more detailed examination of the body-opening of I Thessalonians and subsequently
to the body-opening of the remaining letters.

The disclosure formula in I Thess. 2:1 is the only ostensible body-opening convention in I Thessalonians, though the
section extends through 2:4 and includes a background item.
The formula itself may be cited in full:

> Αὐτοὶ γὰρ οἴδατε, ἀδελφοί, τὴν εἴσοδον ἡμῶν τὴν
> πρὸς ὑμᾶς, ὅτι οὐ κενὴ γέγονεν, ἀλλὰ προπαθόντες
> καὶ ὑβρισθέντες καθὼς οἴδατε ἐν φιλίπποις
> ἐπαρρησιασάμεθα ἐν τῷ θεῷ ἡμῶν λαλῆσαι πρὸς ὑμᾶς
> τὸ εὐαλλέλιον τοῦ θεοῦ ἐν πολλῷ ἀγῶνι.

> "For you yourselves know, brethren, that our visit
> to you was not in vain; but though we had already
> suffered and been shamefully treated at Philippi,
> as you know, we had courage in our God to declare
> to you the gospel of God in the face of great oppo-
> sition."

The "background" item delineating the occasion for Paul's disclosure in 2:1f. is presented subsequently in 2:3f.,[66] where
Paul states why the preaching of the gospel at Thessalonica
was not in vain. Paul's utter dependence on the God (3f.) who
entrusted the gospel to him, is the basis for understanding the
manifestation of power at Thessalonica. The unusual form of
the disclosure formula, i.e., the perfect tense and second
person of the verb meaning "to know," is due to the fact that
Paul's disclosure of what happened is corroborated by the Thessalonians' own knowledge of, and participation in, that event;
a mutual understanding that the gospel was not mere talk but a
manifestation of power exhibited in what both Paul and the Thessalonians "became" on that occasion.[67]

b. Philippians

The second body-opening section to be examined is that of
Phil. 1:12-18. We have two transitional constructions in the
body-opening, the introductory disclosure formula and the formulaic use of interrogative τί, a construction which both closes
the section and functions as a transition to the formal opening
of the body-middle. We may cite the disclosure formula first:

> Γινώσκειν δὲ ὑμᾶς βούλομαι, ἀδελφοί, ὅτι τὰ κατ' ἐμὲ μᾶλλον
> εἰς προκοπὴν τοῦ εὐαγγελίου ἐλήλυθεν, ὥστε τοὺς δεσμούς
> μου φανεροὺς ἐν χριστῷ γενέσθαι ἐν ὅλῳ πραιτωρίῳ καὶ τοῖς
> λοιποῖς πᾶσιν, καὶ τοὺς πλείονας τῶν ἀδελφῶν ἐν κυρίῳ
> πεποιθότας τοῖς δεσμοῖς μου περισσοτέρως τολμᾶν ἀφόβως τὸν
> λόγον τοῦ θεοῦ λαλεῖν.

> "I want you to know, brethren, that what has happened to
> me has really served to advance the gospel, so that it has
> become known throughout the whole praetorian guard and to
> all the rest that my imprisonment is for Christ; and most
> of the brethren have been made confident in the Lord because
> of my imprisonment, and are much more bold to speak the
> word of God without fear."

Paul makes known that what at one time seemed adverse, his imprisonment, has turned out to be an advance. He elaborates
briefly on this disclosure by noting (1:15-17) that the curtail-
ment of his own preaching has acted as an impetus to the more
extensive preaching of the gospel by two opposing groups.[68]
Leaving aside the question of how these groups affect him per-
sonally, Paul turns to the question of their wider significance.
This question, introduced by the interrogative τί, is both the
formulaic means of concluding the body-opening and the means,
because of the language employed, whereby the transition to the
body-middle is executed. In anticipation of the introduction of
the body-middle, this construction may be cited also:

> Τί γάρ; πλὴν ὅτι παντὶ τρόπῳ, εἴτε προφάσει εἴτε ἀληθείᾳ,
> χριστὸς καταγγέλλεται, καὶ ἐν τούτῳ χαίρω·

> "What then? Only that in every way, whether in pretence
> or in truth, Christ is proclaimed; and in that I rejoice."

c. I Corinthians

The next body-opening section to be examined is I Cor. 1:10-
16. The body-opening is introduced in this instance by the request (a device earlier noted in connection with the body-opening
of Philemon):

74

Παρακαλῶ δὲ ὑμᾶς, ἀδελφοί, διὰ τοῦ ὀνόματος τοῦ κυρίου
ἡμῶν Ἰησοῦ Χριστοῦ, ἵνα τὸ αὐτὸ λέγητε πάντες, καὶ μὴ ᾖ
ἐν ὑμῖν σχίσματα, ἦτε δὲ κατηρτισμένοι ἐν τῷ αὐτῷ νοῒ καὶ
ἐν τῇ αὐτῇ γνώμῃ.

"I appeal to you, brethren, by the name of our Lord Jesus
Christ, that all of you agree and that there be no dissen-
sions among you, but that you be united in the same mind
and the same judgment."

Unlike the statement of request in the body-opening of Philemon, the background item--which delineates the circumstances
necessitating the request--does not precede, but follows, the
statement of the request. This background item, though govern-
ing the remaining segment of the body-opening through 1:16, is
begun in 1:11. The introductory segment of this item (containin
γάρ, as background items often do when they succeed their request[69]) is as follows:

ἐδηλώθη γάρ μοι περὶ ὑμῶν, ἀδελφοί, ὑπὸ τῶν Κλόης, ὅτι
ἔριδες ἐν ὑμῖν εἰσιν.

"For it has been reported to me by Chloe's people that
there is quarreling among you, my brethren."

   d. II Corinthians

   The formulaic convention marking the body-opening in II Cor
1:8 is, once again, the disclosure formula. The disclosure formula itself constitutes the largest segment of the body-opening,
though a background item is introduced subsequently in 1:12. We
cite the formula again in order:

Οὐ γὰρ θέλομεν ὑμᾶς ἀγνοεῖν, ἀδελφοί, ὑπὲρ τῆς θλίψεως
ἡμῶν τῆς γενομένης ἐν τῇ Ἀσίᾳ, ὅτι καθ' ὑπερβολὴν ὑπὲρ
δύναμιν ἐβαρήθημεν, ὥστε ἐξαπορηθῆναι ἡμᾶς καὶ τοῦ ζῆν·
ἀλλὰ αὐτοὶ ἐν ἑαυτοῖς τὸ ἀπόκριμα τοῦ θανάτου ἐσχήκαμεν,
ἵνα μὴ πεποιθότες ὦμεν ἐφ' ἑαυτοῖς ἀλλ' ἐπὶ τῷ θεῷ τῷ
ἐγείροντι τοὺς νεκρούς· ὃς ἐκ τηλικούτου θανάτου ἐρρύσατο
ἡμᾶς καὶ ῥύσεται, εἰς ὃν ἠλπίκαμεν καὶ ἔτι ῥύσεται,
συνυπουργούντων καὶ ὑμῶν ὑπὲρ ἡμῶν τῇ δεήσει, ἵνα ἐκ πολλῶν
προσώπων τὸ εἰς ἡμᾶς χάρισμα διὰ πολλῶν εὐχαριστηθῇ ὑπὲρ
ἡμῶν.

"For we do not want you to be ignorant, brethren, of the
afflication we experienced in Asia; for we were so utterly,
unbearably crushed that we despaired of life itself. Why,
we felt that we had received the sentence of death; but that
was to make us rely not on ourselves but on God who raises
the dead; he delivered us from so deadly a peril, and he
will deliver us; on him we have set our hope that he will
deliver us again. You also must help us by prayer, so that
many will give thanks on our behalf for the blessing granted
us in answer to many prayers."

The background item, once again signalled by a γάρ clause, is confined to one verse which closes the body-opening.

᾽Η γάρ καύχησις ἡμῶν αὕτη ἐστίν, τὸ μαρτύριον τῆς συνειδήσεως ἡμῶν, ὅτι ἐν ἁγιότητι καὶ εἰλικρινείᾳ τοῦ θεοῦ, οὐκ ἐν σοφίᾳ σαρκικῇ ἀλλ᾽ ἐν χάριτι θεοῦ, ἀνεστράφημεν ἐν τῷ κόσμῳ, περισσοτέρως δὲ πρὸς ὑμᾶς.[70]

"For our boast is this, the testimony of our conscience that we have behaved in the world, and still more toward you, with holiness and godly sincerity, not by earthly wisdom but by the grace of God."

e. Philippians 4:10-20

The final passage to come into consideration as a body-opening section is Phil. 4:10-13. This reference has been reserved to the last because it constitutes a problem in analysis which did not arise in the preceding sections. I have sought methodologically to analyze only those portions of the seven Pauline letters which are circumscribed by body-opening and body-closing formulae. Though more of these four letters than Philippians may be composite, I have ventured to analyze only Phil. 4:10-20 as an example of an independent letter, both because, in my opinion, this passage presents more identifiable features of the body-opening and the body-closing, and because the extension of these formal criteria to the entirety of the four letters lies beyond the purview of this study.[71]

Apart from the fact that 4:10-20 introduces a new subject, we find an expression of joy in 4:10, a formula which is often employed in the papyri, and once elsewhere in Paul, to open the body of the letter. We may note also that the section from 4:14-20 corresponds roughly to the apostolic *parousia* (the body-closing) section. "This may...be an independent letter, now truncated."[72]

We may cite this body-opening formula (which corresponds closely to the body-opening joy expression in Philem. 7) and take up the question of the apostolic *parousia* section subsequently:

᾽Εχάρην δὲ ἐν κυρίῳ μεγάλως ὅτι ἤδη ποτὲ ἀνεθάλετε τὸ ὑπὲρ ἐμοῦ φρονεῖν· ἐφ᾽ ᾧ καὶ ἐφρονεῖτε, ἠκαιρεῖσθε δέ.

"I rejoice in the Lord greatly that now at length you have revived your concern for me; you were indeed concerned for me, but you had no opportunity."

3. *Body-Middle*

    a. I Thessalonians

    The body-middle of I Thessalonians, sketched roughly earlier
may now be taken up in greater detail. Though the section extends formally from 2:5-16, we will find it helpful to abstract
the major transitional formulae in order from 2:1-16.

> 2:1f.   Αὐτοὶ γὰρ οἴδατε, ἀδελφοί,...οὐ κενὴ γέγονεν
>   (ἡ. εἴσοδος ἡμῶν ἡ πρὸς ὑμᾶς),...καθὼς οἴδατε...
>   λαλῆσαι πρὸς ὑμᾶς τὸ εὐαγγέλιον...ἐν πολλῷ
>   ἀγῶνι.
>
> 2:5ff.   οὔτε γὰρ...ἐν λόγῳ κολακείας ἐγενήθημεν, καθὼς
>   οἴδατε,...ἀλλὰ ἐγενήθημεν... διότι ἀγαπητοὶ
>   ἡμῖν ἐγενήθητε.
>
> 2:9   μνημονεύετε γάρ, ἀδελφοί, τὸν κόπον ἡμῶν...
>
> 2:10ff. ὑμεῖς μάρτυρες...ὡς ὁσίως...ὑμῖν...ἐγενήθημεν,
>   καθάπερ οἴδατε...
>
> 2:13   Καὶ διὰ τοῦτο καὶ ἡμεῖς εὐχαριστοῦμεν...
>
> 2:14f.   ὑμεῖς γὰρ μιμηταὶ ἐγενήθητε, ἀδελφοί,...
>   καθὼς καὶ αὐτοί...

The entire section from 2:1-16 is organized around two
formulaic features, the use of the aorist passive form of γίνομαι
(either ἐγενήθημεν or ἐγενήθητε, except for the use of γέγονεν
in 2:1) and the two-membered concatenation καθὼς (or καθάπερ)
οἴδατε. The body-middle section of I Thessalonians, therefore,
like the body-middle of Galatians and Romans, is characterized
by a discrete construction, integrally connected to the message
of the body. The form of the body-opening disclosure formula
itself, in this case, telegraphs the subsequent character of the
body-middle. We may now take up in order the analysis of the
two principal divisions of the body-middle.

    Part I of the body-middle extends from 2:5-12 and may be
divided at the two major points of transition, the introductory
formula of the section at 2:5 and the transition at 2:9 and 2:10ff
The background section of the body-opening (2:3f.) provided a
partial explanation for the success of the gospel, disclosed in
2:1, when it was preached at Thessalonica. The formula which
opens the body-middle in 2:5, and extends through 2:8, develops
the explanation stated in 2:3f. in greater detail. Paul asserts
here that he could have made certain claims on the Thessalonians
because of his office as an apostle. The fact that he did not
make despotic commands, but voluntarily placed himself under
obligation to the claims of the gospel, reveals that he himself
lives life as a gift from God. What "happened" as a consequence

is set forth in three clauses, each marked by the use of the verb
γίνομαι:

(i) οὔτε ... ἐν λόγῳ κολακείας ἐγενήθημεν, 2:5 ("Our words
have never *been* flattering words," NEB);

(ii) ἀλλὰ ἐγενήθημεν ἤπιοι ἐν μέσῳ ὑμῶν..., 2:7b ("But we
were gentle among you,";)

(iii) διότι ἀγαπητοὶ ἡμῖν ἐγενήθητε, 2:8b ("because you had
become very dear to us.")

The next major point in the development of Part I is 2:9.
This transition may be identified by the use of the vocative,
ἀδελφοί. The force of this transition is strengthened in 2:10
by the repetition of the two principal formulaic items of this
section, the aorist passive form of γίνομαι and καθάπερ οἴδατε.

Part II of the body-middle of I Thessalonians, 2:13-16,
was taken up in some detail previously. It will be unnecessary
at this point, therefore, to reiterate either the nature of the
formula which introduces the section or the explanation regarding
why the section may be regarded as the applicative side of the
body-middle. We may note in passing, however, that a second
point of transition within Part II ensues at 2:14 and is marked
by the use both of the vocative and the formulaic form of
γίνομαι (the aorist passive) found elsewhere in the body-middle.[73]

b. Philippians

The body-middle of Philippians extends from 1:18b-2:18,
rounded off by an "eschatological climax" in 2:14-18. Something
of the flavor of the body-middle is telegraphed, we noted, in
the formula which concludes the body-opening. Both this formula
and the more significant points of transition within the body-
middle may be outlined in order that the particular formulaic
nuance of the body-middle of Philippians may be illustrated.

1:18   τί γάρ; ...παντὶ τρόπῳ,...Χριστὸς καταγγέλλεται,
        καὶ ἐν τούτῳ χαίρω· (What then?...in every way,...
        Christ is proclaimed; and in that I rejoice.")

1:25   καὶ τοῦτο πεποιθὼς οἶδα, ὅτι μενῶ...εἰς τὴν ὑμῶν
        προκοπὴν καὶ χαρὰν τῆς πίστεως, ("Convinced of
        this, I know that I shall remain...for your pro-
        gress and joy in the faith.")

1:27   Μόνον ἀξίως τοῦ εὐαγγελίου...πολιτεύεσθε,...
        ("only let your manner of life be worthy of the
        gospel...")

2:1   Εἴ τις οὖν παράκλησις...πληρώσατέ μου τὴν χαρὰν...
        ("So if there is any encouragement...complete my
        joy...")

2:12   "Ὥστε, ἀγαπητοί μου,...τὴν ἑαυτῶν σωτηρίαν
κατεργάζεσθε· ("Therefore, my beloved,... work
out your own salvation...")

2:17   'Αλλὰ εἰ καὶ σπένδομαι..., χαίρω καὶ συγχαίρω
πᾶσιν ὑμῖν· τὸ δὲ αὐτὸ καὶ ὑμεῖς χαίρετε καὶ
συγχαίρετέ μοι. ("Even if I am to be poured as a
libation...,I am glad and rejoice with you all.
Likewise you also should be glad and rejoice
with me.")

Five of the seven points of transition outlined above employ either the verb χαίρω or its cognate noun χαρά. We may be
reasonably safe in concluding, as a number of interpreters do,
therefore, that a tone of joy sounds throughout. The letter
may be characterized also by another formulaic expression, only
intimated in the body-middle, the perfect form of the verb πείθω
(1:25). The recognition of this latter item will better enable
us to interpret the joy expressions.[74]

We may assume, on the basis of 1:12-18, that Paul's pre-
eminent concern during his imprisonment was the success of the
gospel. But within what ostensibly appears a situation of de-
feat and despair, his own imprisonment, he has found that the
gospel is not thwarted. On the contrary, his experiences have
taught him precisely how it is that one must stand before the
gospel, i.e., one must put his confidence in its message even
in the face of death. This fundamental confidence is the basis
for true joy, a joy not defeated by circumstance. This interpretation lends greater weight to the thesis earlier suggested
regarding the role and interpretation of the "confidence formula"
in the body-closing,[75] i.e., Paul's basis of confidence is vested
not primarily in his addressees but in the ultimate success of
the gospel. With these general observations before us, therefore, we may now turn to an analysis of the two divisions of
the body-middle.

The first part of the body-middle, Paul's *apologia*, extends
from 1:18b-26 and contains two principal transitions. Both of
these formulaic transitions employ the verb χαίρω (or the cognate
χαρά) and a disclosure formula (in both cases the form is οἶδα).
The first of these two formulae opens Part I in 1:18bff., and
the latter formally closes the section in 1:25f.

The more practical segment of the body-middle, extends from
1:27-2:18. The four principal points of transition in this section (1:27; 2:1,12,17), apart from the use of the verb χαίρω in
2:17 and the cognate χαρά in 2:1, evidence little similarity with
each other.[76] The section is initiated in 1:27 by the imperative.

The transition immediately following (2:1) is also introduced by
the imperative. The third point of transition, introduced by
Ὥστε in 2:12, is the resolution of the points scored within the
two preceding segments of Part II. It is the formal conclusion,
therefore, of the section. Paul proceeds in 2:14-18, nonetheless, to reiterate what is demanded of the Philippians, but in
relation to the coming day of the Lord. These verses set forth
an eschatological conclusion which, according to Robert Funk,[77]
corresponds to the eschatological climax that Paul Schubert identified as the conclusion of the thanksgiving period.

c. I Corinthians

The body-middle of I Corinthians is introduced in 1:17 and,
like Philippians, is formally concluded with an eschatological
climax, extending from 4:1-13. Both the intricacy of the theological argument itself as well as the diversity of its expression make this letter-body difficult to reduce to a schematic
pattern. We will attempt to sketch the major points of transition, nonetheless, in order to catch something of the flavor of
the argument.

1:17   οὐ γὰρ ἀπέστειλέν με Χριστὸς βαπτίζειν ἀλλὰ
        εὐαγγελίζεσθαι, οὐκ ἐν σοφίᾳ λόγου, ἵνα μὴ κενωθῇ
        ὁ σταυρὸς τοῦ Χριστοῦ. ("For Christ did not send
        me to baptize but to preach the gospel, and not
        with eloquent wisdom, lest the cross of Christ
        be emptied of its power.")

                                    (1) τ. μὲν ἀπολλυμένοις
1:18   Ὁ λόγος...τοῦ σταυροῦ   μωρία ἐσ.
                                    (2) τ. δὲ σῳζομένοις..δύναμις
                                        θεοῦ ἐστιν.[78]
2:1f.   Κἀγὼ.., ἀδελφοί, ἦλθον   (1) οὐ καθ᾽ ὑπεροχὴν λόγου
                                        ἢ σοφίας καταγγέλλων...
                                    (2) οὐ γὰρ..εἰδέναι..εἰ μὴ
                                        Ἰησ. Χριστὸν,..
                                        ἐσταυρωμένον.[79]
                                    (1) ὁ λόγος μου..οὐκ ἐν..
2:3ff. Κἀγὼ..ἐγενόμην..καὶ   σοφίας λόγοις,
                                    (2) ἀλλ᾽ ἐν ἀποδείξει
                                        πνεύματος καὶ δυνάμεως,[80]
2:7ff. ἀλλὰ λαλοῦμεν θεοῦ σοφίαν ἐν μυστηρίῳ...
            (1) ἣν προώρισεν ὁ θεὸς πρὸ τ. αἰώνων...
            (2) ἣν οὐδεὶς τ. ἀρχόντων...ἔγνωκεν·
            (2΄) εἰ γὰρ ἔγνωσαν, οὐκ ἄν...ἐσταύρωσαν·
            (1΄) ἡμῖν..ἀπεκάλυψεν ὁ θεὸς διὰ τ. πνεύματος[81]
2:13ff. ἃ καὶ λαλοῦμεν
            (1) οὐκ ἐν...σοφίας λόγοις,
            (2) ἀλλ᾽ ἐν διδακτοῖς πνεύματος,
            (1΄) ψυχικὸς δὲ ἄνθρωπος...
            (2΄) ὁ δὲ πνευματικὸς...

3:1ff. Κἀγώ, ἀδελφοί, οὐκ ἠδυνήθην λαλῆσαι ὑμῖν ὡς
πνευματ. ...[82]

3:5 Τί οὖν ἐστιν 'Α.; ("What then is Apollos?")

3:16 Οὐκ οἴδατε ὅτι ναὸς θεοῦ..: ("Do you not know that
you are God's temple?")

3:18 Μηδεὶς ἑαυτὸν ἐξαπατάτω· ("Let no one deceive
himself.")

3:21 ὥστε μηδεὶς καυχάσθω ἐν ἀνθρώποις·[83]

4:1 Οὕτως ἡμᾶς λογιζέσθω ἄνθρωπος ὡς ὑπηρέτας...("This
is how one should regard us, as servants...")

4:6 Ταῦτα δέ, ἀδελφοί, μετεσχημάτισα εἰς ἐμαυτὸν καὶ
'Α. δι' ὑμᾶς,...("I have applied all this to myself
and Apollos for your benefit, brethren,...")

One may note that each point of transition within the section from 1:17-3:1--which includes all of Part I of the body-
middle and the introductory formula to Part II (3:1)--is characterized by an emphasis on "speaking." This "speaking" is presented, at least in 1:17-2:13ff., in a dialectical form; one type
of speaking, characterized primarily by the words σοφία λόγου,
is set over against another form of speaking, variously defined
as μωρία (ἀσθενές, ἀγενής, ἐξουθενημένος), δύναμις, διδακτός
πνεύματος.

The first segment of the body-middle (Part I) is introduced
in 1:17 and ends at 2:16. Though it does not appear to play a
major role elsewhere within the body, οὐ γάρ is employed to introduce the body-middle in 1:17.[84] It is hardly fortuitous that
the same construction is employed in Rom. 1:16 to introduce the
body-middle. This construction is also in II Cor. 1:8, though
it is employed there in the body-opening statement. The identification of I Cor. 1:17 as the point of transition to the body-
middle is strengthened, in any case, by the analogous use of
οὐ γάρ in Romans.

The problem of factions was taken up in the body-opening
in relation both to the crucifixion and to baptism. These
items are reiterated in 1:17, but only one of the items (σταυρός,
"cross") is thematically developed within the body. One may
even question whether the subject of the cross is consistently
developed, i.e., whereas the cross is contrasted with the Corinthian factions in the body-opening, its antithesis in the body-
middle is σοφία λόγου. Ulrich Wilckens renders this otherwise
inexplicable transition to the discussion of sophia intelligible
by relating it specifically to the problem of Corinthian factious-
ness.[85]

Taking Wilcken's suggestion (i.e., that the use of sophia is related to the problem of factions) as our point of departure, we may observe that in each of the six points of transition within Part I of the body-middle, Paul contrasts the manner of speaking accruing to the cross with the manner of speaking which the Corinthian factions represent.

These initial observations suggest that Paul is not refer- ring to "speaking" or "words" in a discursive sense. Robert Funk demonstrates precisely this point in an analysis of I Cor. 2:6-16, alleging that we have to do here not with speaking in words "but in the sense of event."[86] The proof of this thesis is formally intimated at two principal points within Part I (the transitions at 2:1 and 2:3: Κἀγὼ.., ἀδελφοί, ἦλθον and Κἀγὼ...ἐγενόμην), where Paul describes the manner of speaking (i.e., how he "came" or "became") in which he evangelized the Corinthians.

The more applicative segment of the body-middle (Part II) is introduced in 3:1 by a formula reiterating the theme of speak- ing. This segment is concluded by the eschatological climax which extends from 4:1-13. The major transitional import of 3:1 is substantiated not only by the reference to speaking (λαλῆσαι) but also by the repetition of κἀγώ and the presence of the vo- cative.

The resolution of the argument in 3:21-23, introduced by ὥστε, is succeeded by an eschatological period in 4:1-13. This same pattern, i.e., the resolution of the argument introduced by ὥστε, followed by an eschatological conclusion, was exhibited also in Philippians.

d. II Corinthians

We anticipate the initiation of the body-middle of II Cor- inthians in 1:13, since the body-opening section concludes with the background item in 1:12. But the section of the letter that extends from 1:13-22 actually bears all the marks of a body-closing section. Indeed, we find two additional body- closing sections in the first seven chapters of II Corinthians! For the sake of illustration, these "body-closing" sections are outlined in sequence below, according to the three-fold pattern of body-closing formulae previously delineated (i.e., a=the motivation for writing formula; b=the confidence phrase; c=the implementation of the apostolic parousia).

(1) a. (1:13)   οὐ γὰρ ἄλλα γράφομεν ὑμῖν ἀλλ᾽ ἢ ἃ
ἀναγινώσκετε
"For we write you nothing but what you can read..."

b. (1:15a)   Καὶ ταύτῃ τῇ πεποιθήσει
"Because I was sure of this..."

c. (1:15ff.)ἐβουλόμην πρότερον πρὸς ὑμᾶς ἐλθεῖν ἵνα...
χάριν σχῆτε,...88

(2) c. (1:23-2:2) ᾿Εγὼ δὲ μάρτυρα τ. θεὸν ἐπικαλοῦμαι..,
ὅτι φειδόμενος ὑμῶν οὐκέτι ἦλθον εἰς Κόρινθον.
"But I call God to witness..., it was to spare you
that I refrained from coming to Corinth."

a. (2:3)   καὶ ἔγραψα τοῦτο αὐτὸ ἵνα μὴ ἐλθὼν λύπην
σχῶ...
"And I wrote as I did, so that when I came I might
not be pained..."

b. (2.3b)   πεποιθὼς ἐπὶ πάντας ὑμᾶς ὅτι...
"For I felt sure of all of you, that..."

a' (2:4)   ἐκ γὰρ πολλῆς θλίψεως...ἔγραψα ὑμῖν...,οὐχ
ἵνα λυπηθῆτε, ἀλλὰ τ. ἀγάπην ἵνα γνῶτε ἣν ἔχω...
"For I wrote you out of much affliction..., not to
cause you pain but to let you know the abundant love
that I have for you."

a''(2:9)   εἰς τοῦτο γὰρ καὶ ἔγραψα, ἵνα...
"For this is why I wrote, that I might..."

c. (2:12)   ᾿Ελθὼν δὲ εἰς τὴν Τρῳάδα...οὐκ ἔσχηκα
ἄνεσιν...μὴ εὑρεῖν με Τίτον τ. ἀδελφόν μου,...
"When I came to Troas...(my mind) could not rest
because I did not find my brother Titus there."

a'''(3:2)   ἡ ἐπιστολὴ ἡμῶν ὑμεῖς ἐστε,...
"You yourselves are our letter of recommendation,..."

b' (3:4)   Πεποίθησιν δὲ τοιαύτην ἔχομεν διὰ τ.
Χριστοῦ πρὸς τ. θεόν...
"Such is the confidence that we have through Christ
toward God."

(3) a. (7:3)   πρὸς κατάκρισιν οὐ λέγω· προείρηκα γὰρ
ὅτι ἐν τ. καρδίαις ἡμῶν...
"I do not say this to condemn you, for I said before
that you are in our hearts...."

b. (7:4)   πολλή μοι παρρησία πρὸς ὑμᾶς,...
"I have great confidence in you;..."

c. (7:5-16) καὶ γὰρ ἐλθόντων ἡμῶν εἰς Μακεδονίαν
οὐδεμίαν ἔσχηκεν ἄνεσιν...
"For even when we came into Macedonia, (our bodies)
had no rest..."

All three formulaic units of the body-closing are employed
at least once within each of these three "body-closing" segments.
It seems very unlikely, therefore, that the presence and sequence
of these formulaic units is accidental. What can we make of
this strange state of affairs? Do these body-closing sections
represent three independent letter fragments? Or, is Paul him-

self responsible for this unusual concatenation of body-closing
sections? The first two body-closing sections, which attach
directly to the body-opening, are out of order in any view since
no body-middle section has been introduced at this point in the
letter.

With regard to the composition of II Corinthians 1-7, Günther Bornkamm has suggested that we have two independent letters:
(1) 1:8-2:13 + 7:5-16 (Paul's account of his anxious journey from
Asia to Macedonia, the so-called "Letter of reconciliation");
(2) 2:14-7:4 (the great "defense" of the apostolic ministry of
Paul).[89] Though Bornkamm's thesis accounts for the points of
greatest disjunction within these seven chapters, i.e., the il-
logical transition from 2:13 to 2:14 and the transition from
7:4 to 7:5, a number of formal problems remain. We find that
all three of the body-closing sections identified above, on the
basis of Bornkamm's division, fall within the limits of letter
1 (i.e., 1:8-2:13 + 7:5-16) whereas letter 2 (i.e., 2:14-7:4)
has *no* body-closing section. Letter 2 is at best a letter fragment, on formal grounds, resembling what has been previously
identified as body-middle. We have in these seven chapters,
then, a body-opening, three body-closing sections, and perhaps
a body-middle.

On the basis of just such formal data, Robert Funk has suggested that these first seven chapters of II Corinthians may
actually constitute a unity.[90] He accounts for the reversal of
the body-middle and the body-closing, on the one hand, and the
number of body-closing sections (he suggests, however, that
there are *two* such sections), on the other, in the following
way: "A second glance suggests that the letter of reconciliation may be a travelogue[91] without a body. Is it possible that
chapters 1-7 are a unity after all, with a travelogue enclosing
the body of the letter precisely as is the case with Romans?"[92]

We have another example, therefore, of a phenomenon we
found in I Thessalonians, the expanded use of one element (the
"apostolic *parousia*" here) to the exclusion or blurring of another (the body-middle). Not only does the apostolic *parousia*
(body-closing) play a predominant role in II Corinthians, it
actually swallows up the body-middle. Though the body-middle
(2:14-7:4) contains major identifiable transitions characteristic of the epistolary situation, these transitions have no

independent identity. The same nuances which shape the apostolic
parousia are taken up in 2:14-7:4.[93] The very subject of this
body-middle, the nature of Paul's apostolic office, is a theme
which logically belongs to the body-closing. An expanded apostolic *parousia*, both legitimating and defining Paul's role as
an apostle, therefore, *is* the message of the body.

4. *Body-Closing*

Though five body-closing sections may be adduced at this
point, it will be necessary to investigate only three in detail.
The body-closing of II Corinthians was analyzed in the immediately preceding section in relation to the body-middle and, therefore, does not need to be analyzed anew. The body-closing of
the truncated letter in Phil. 4:10-20--though a review of Paul's
presence in Philippi and possibly a surrogate for the apostolic
parousia--lacks the formal items which could be subjected to
analysis. The three remaining body-closing references are:
I Thess. 2:17-3:18; Phil. 2:19-30; and I Cor. 4:14-21.

Due to some degree of similarity in form and an even greater
similarity of structure, the three formulae are illustrated on
the following page in Table 2 (just as the body-closing formulae
of Philemon, Galatians, and Romans were set out in Table 1 on
page 61). The first two formulae of the body-closing, i.e., the
motivation for writing-responsibility formula and the confidence
phrase, are diagrammed (cf. Table 2 on the following page) according to the structural model earlier proposed (cf. Table I,
61). Due to the extensive length and lack of consistent order
of items within the *final* formulaic unit of the body-closing,
Robert Funk's symbols for these will be presented in Table 2
instead of a descriptive outline.

a. The Motivation for Writing-Responsibility Formula

The nature of the three formal items of the motivation for
writing formula, first set forth in Table 1 on page 61, may be
briefly reiterated: (i) a formulaic statement of authorship
(ἐγὼ Παῦλος); (ii) reference to the act of writing (γράφω); and
(iii) reiteration of the reason for writing (introduced by various means, cf. item (3) in Table 1 and comments on page 62f.).
With regard to the first formulaic unit in the body-closing of
I Thessalonians, Philippians, and I Corinthians, we may note

TABLE 2.--STRUCTURAL UNITS IN THE APOSTOLIC *PAROUSIA* OF I THESSALONIANS, PHILIPPIANS, & I CORINTHIANS

Motivation for Writing-Responsibility Formula

	Item (1)	Item (2)	Item (3)
I Th.2:17-19	Ἡμεῖς δέ, ἀδελφοί,	διότι ἠθελήσαμεν ἐλθεῖν πρὸς ὑμᾶς	ἐσπουδάσαμεν τ.πρόσωπον ὑμῶν ἰδεῖν..
Phil.2:19-23	ἐγὼ μὲν Παῦλος... κἀγὼ	'Ελπίζω...Τ. ταχέως πέμψαι ὑμῖν,	ἵνα (κἀγὼ) εὐψυχῶ(γνοὺς τὰ)περὶ ὑμῶν.
I Cor.4:14f.	ἐγὼ ὑμᾶς ἐγέννησα	ὑμᾶς γράφω ταῦτα,	Οὐκ ἐντρέπων ἀλλ' ὡς τέκνα...ἀγαπητὰ νουθετῶν·

Confidence Formula

	Item			
I Th.2:19f, Phil.2:24	...ἡμῶν καὶ αὐτὸς	ἐλπὶς ἢ χαρὰ ἢ... πέποιθα δὲ	οὐχὶ καὶ ὑμεῖς... ἐν κυρίῳ	ὑμεῖς γὰρ ἐστε ἡ δόξα... ὅτι (καὶ αὐτὸς) ταχέως ἐλεύσομαι
I Cor.4:16	μου	παρακαλῶ οὖν		μιμηταί (μου) γίνεσθε

Implementation of the Apostolic *Parousia*

I Thess. 2:17-3:13				Phil. 2:19-24		I Cor. 4:14-21			
3a	17b;cf.3:6b	4a(3f)	3:10a	3e	19-23	1a	14	5b	18, 19b-21
3b	18a	5b	3:10b	5a	19b	2	15-16		
3c	18b;cf.2:16	4a	3:11	3f	24	3e	17		
3e	3:2-5					3f	19a		
5a	3:6-9					4b	19a		

(Table 2, page 85) that items (2) and (3) fail to evidence similarity from letter to letter and fail, by and large, to correspond formally to the same items in Philemon, Galatians, and
Romans (Table 1, page 61).

We must take up each of these letters individually in order
to indicate how the requirements of each of these three items
are met.

    a. I Thessalonians

We take up the first formulaic unit in relation to the body-
closing of I Thessalonians, which begins at 2:17:

> Ἡμεῖς δέ, ἀδελφοί, ἀπορφανισθέντες ἀφ' ὑμῶν πρὸς καιρὸν
> ὥρας προσώπῳ οὐ καρδίᾳ, περισσοτέρως ἐσπουδάσαμεν τὸ
> πρόσωπον ὑμῶν ἰδεῖν ἐν πολλῇ ἐπιθυμίᾳ. διότι ἠθελήσαμεν
> ἐλθεῖν πρὸς ὑμᾶς, ἐγὼ μὲν Παῦλος καὶ ἅπαξ καὶ δίς, καὶ
> ἐνέκοψεν ἡμᾶς ὁ σατανᾶς.

> "But since we were bereft of you, brethren, for a short
> time, in person not in heart, we endeavored the more eager-
> ly and with great desire to see you face to face; because
> we wanted to come to you--I, Paul, again and again--but
> Satan hindered us."

The occasion for writing suggested earlier was Paul's desire to
share with the Thessalonians the thanksgiving he felt toward
God for what had "happened" at Thessalonica. In the interim
between that occasion and Timothy's return visit from the Thessalonians, Paul had suffered many anxious moments. Indeed, Paul's
joy and thankfulness is so great when he hears Timothy's report
that his thankfulness cannot be adequately expressed via letter
(cf. the above quotation). On this basis, we may understand why
Paul refers to his desire to visit the Thessalonians in item
(2) of the first formulaic unit of the body-closing (cf. Table
2, page 85) rather than to the act of writing. We may also
understand item (3) of this first formulaic unit on the same
basis, i.e., the reason Paul wants to visit the Thessalonians
(cf. item (3) in I Thessalonians in Table 2) is that he may
express his thankfulness face to face. The occasion for the
letter, therefore, is not primarily the "written" thankfulness
but the announcement of a visit whereby Paul may more accurately
convey his thanks himself. This state of affairs is further
substantiated in 3:9: "For what thanksgiving can we render to
God for you, for all the joy which we feel for your sake before
our God, praying earnestly night and day that we may see you face
to face and supply what is lacking in your faith?"

b. Philippians

The first formulaic unit of the body-closing of Phil. 2:19-
23 is, if possible, even more suspect in relation to formal features than the parallel in I Thessalonians. Not one of the three
items of this first unit bears a distinct resemblance to the model
derived from Philemon, Galatians, and Romans. Dissimilarity of
formal items notwithstanding, the passage functions structurally
in a way comparable to the motivation for writing formula in the
other letters. We may cite the segment of the body-closing
functionally comparable to the formulaic unit.

Ἐλπίζω δὲ ἐν κυρίῳ Ἰησοῦ Τιμόθεον ταχέως πέμψαι ὑμῖν,
ἵνα κἀγὼ εὐψυχῶ γνοὺς τὰ περὶ ὑμῶν. ...τοῦτον μὲν οὖν ἐλπίζω
πέμψαι ὡς ἂν ἀφίδω τὰ περὶ ἐμὲ ἐξαυτῆς·

"I hope in the Lord Jesus to send Timothy to you soon,
so that I may be cheered by news of you. ...I hope therefore to send him just as soon as I see how it will go with
me;"

Both this reference and the passage analyzed immediately above
in I Thessalonians have been tabulated in Robert Funk's study as
items in the implementation of the apostolic *parousia* section,
i.e., the *final* formulaic unit in the body-closing. The unusual
form of the first unit of the body-closing of I Thessalonians,
we noted above, is due to the peculiar nature of the epistolary
situation. Do we find an analogous explanation for the unusual
form of the first body-closing unit in Philippians?

Many interpreters have assumed that Philippins is Paul's
letter of thanks to the Philippians for the money which had been
sent through Epaphroditas. Paul Schubert modified this assumption slightly, however, by suggesting that Paul's "joy" arises
not so much over a recent money gift as over the evidence it
furnishes of the Philippians' cooperation in the gospel.[94]
There are points within the letter, however, where we are made
aware that the Philippians are not the primary basis, on either
view, of Paul's joy or confidence. The basis of Paul's joy, as
suggested earlier (77f.), is his belief, strengthened by the
imprisonment, that the gospel will succeed despite circumstance.
The Philippians evidence a participation in the gospel but Paul
intimates (1:24f.) that they, nonetheless, lack the "joy which
comes from faith" that sustains him. They are deficient enough
that at one point Paul's projected visit to the Philippians
should be regarded as a threat:

> "My desire is to depart and be with Christ,... But to
> remain in the flesh is more necessary on your account.
> Convinced of this, I know that I shall remain..for your
> progress and joy in the faith, so that in me you may have
> ample cause to glory in Christ Jesus, because of my coming
> to you again." (1:23b-26)[95]

Even the mention of Ephaphroditus in the body-closing ought,
probably, to be viewed in the light of some problem at Philippi.
Obviously, he was returning earlier than anticipated, since the
Philippians had expressly sent him to remain in Paul's company.[96]
The "necessity" (ἀναγκαῖον, 2:25) for his return probably corres-
ponds to the "more necessary" (ἀναγκαιότερεν, 1:24) reason why
Paul himself must remain for the Philippians.[97]

On this basis, therefore, the desire to send Timothy--sug-
gested as item (2) in the first unit of the body-closing (cf.
Table 2)--is consistent both with the motivation for writing expressed elsewhere in the body and with the *reason* for sending
him expressed in item (3) of the first body-closing unit (cf.
Table 2), i.e., Paul has written the Philippians via Epaphroditus
to alert them in advance of Timothy's coming visit.

c. I Corinthians

The first body-closing unit in I Corinthians, unlike Philippians and I Thessalonians, maintains a rather formal identity
with the form of the formula proposed in connection with Philemon
Galatians, and Romans. The only real problem is the sequence of
items (note the reversal in the order of items in Table 2). This
particular aspect of the formulaic unit does not warrant an explanation, in my opinion, however, since it seems unnecessary to
expect Paul to follow his constructs woodenly. Laying the sequence of items aside, we now turn to the demonstration of the
formal similarity of the individual items with parallel items in
Philemon, Galatians, and Romans.

The formulaic statement of authorship (cf. item (1) in the
first body-closing unit of Table 2), like Philemon, Galatians,
and Romans, is conveyed through the use of the emphatic pronoun,
ἐγώ. Similarly, the second item of this formulaic unit conforms
to the model previously derived from the study of Philemon,
Galatians, and Romans, since Paul explicitly refers to the act
of writing (γράφω here). The third item within this unit, as
the corresponding item elsewhere, conveys the reason for writing

(cf. item (3) in Table 2: Οὐκ ἐντρέπων..., ἀλλ' ὡς τέκνα μου
ἀγαπητὰ νουθετῶν, "not...to make you ashamed, but to admonish
you as my beloved children").[98]

b. The Confidence Formula

The second formulaic unit within the body-closing, like the
first, does not follow the conventional phraseology previously
established in connection with this unit. The sole exception
here is the Philippian reference which follows the pattern rather
faithfully. We may facilitate the investigation at this point,
perhaps, by briefly reviewing the four formal items within this
second boy-closing unit: (1) the emphatic form of the pronoun,
ἐγώ; (2) the perfect form of the verb πείθω, the means by which
Paul alleges his "confidence"; (3) specification of the basis of
confidence, defined as residing either in the Lord or in Paul's
addressees; (4) the statement of the object concerning which
Paul is confident, introduced by ὅτι. In order to demonstrate
the functional identity of the second formulaic unit in the three
letters before us with the parallel unit in the other Pauline
letters, we take up the letters once again individually.

a. I Thessalonians

We may better understand how I Thess. 2:19f. is a surrogate
for the confidence formula, perhaps, by setting forth the passage
in its entirety.

> τίς γὰρ ἡμῶν ἐλπὶς ἢ χαρὰ ἢ στέφανος καυχήσεως--ἢ οὐχὶ καὶ
> ὑμεῖς--ἔμπροσθεν τοῦ κυρίου ἡμῶν Ἰησοῦ ἐν τῇ αὐτοῦ
> παρουσίᾳ; ὑμεῖς γάρ ἐστε ἡ δόξα ἡμῶν καὶ ἡ χαρά.

> "For what is our hope or joy or crown of boasting before
> our Lord Jesus at his coming? Is it not you? For you
> are our glory and joy."

The basis for the confidence regularly affirmed in Paul's letters--
a confidence even formalized into a structural unit within the
letter--is his trust in the victorious termination of the gospel.
We find this kind of confidence implicit in the above phrase
"boasting before our Lord Jesus at his coming." An additional
aspect of this trust in the gospel, expressed in each of the
seven letters examined, is Paul's belief that the gospel will
prove successful in the concrete situations of the churches to
which he writes. The evidence of the gospel's success, in relation to the Thessalonian congregation, is reflected in the

stance which the Thessalonians have taken in response to the
preaching of the gospel, a theme running throughout I Thessalonians and the basis for Paul's thanksgiving to God. Having established the general sense in which I Thessalonians embodies
the confidence formula in the body-closing, we may now work at
the functional correspondence between individual items.

The second item of the confidence phrase, the *statement*
of confidence, finds its surrogate in I Thessalonians in the
words: ἐλπὶς ἤ χαρὰ ἤ στέφανος καυχήσεως...ἔμπροσθεν τοῦ κυρίου
ἡμῶν 'Ιησοῦ ἐν τῇ αὐτοῦ παρουσίᾳ,"(our) hope or joy or crown of
boasting before our Lord Jesus at his coming."[99] The statement
of confidence is couched in this form because it does not have
the future orientation, which we find elsewhere in the Pauline
letters. In this instance, the Thessalonians' *present* manner
of life substantiates Paul's basis of confidence. Similarly,
the specification of the basis of Paul's confidence (cf. the
third item in the confidence formula in Table 2) is the Thessalonians themselves, since they are living proof of the victorious
nature of the gospel. Finally, the explicit reference of the
object concerning which Paul is confident (the fourth item in
the confidence formula, cf. Table 2) has its parallel in Paul's
statement: "For you are our glory and joy."

b. Philippians

The confidence formula conforms to the pattern very well in
the letter to the Philippians, lacking only the emphatic pronoun (the first item of the formula): item (2) is the perfect
form of πείθω (see Table 2); item (3) specifies the "Lord" as
Paul's basis of confidence; and the object concerning which
Paul is confident--his coming visit here--is introduced by ὅτι
in item (4). We may now interpret the meaning of this second
body-closing formula in the light of the comments suggested
in connection with the opening unit. The gravity of the problem at Philippi, as suggested earlier, is, perhaps, the reason
why Paul intends to send Timothy in the near future and
Epaphroditus at the present. Is the severity of the problem
also the reason why Paul is confident that he himself will be
allowed to visit the Philippians, i.e., is he so confident in
the gospel's power that he does not believe the situation at
Philippi could continue unrelieved?

c. I Corinthians

The peculiar form of the confidence formula in I Corinthians
is tied, once again, to the nature of the epistolary situation.
This unit may be cited at the start:

παρακαλῶ οὖν ὑμᾶς, μιμηταί μου γίνεσθε. ("I urge you,
then, be imitators of me," I Cor. 4:16)

The occasion prompting the message of I Cor. 1-4, as suggested previously, was the "manner of speaking" which characterized the Corinthians. Whereas Paul and the other apostles spoke
as men stamped by the cross, i.e., as men who lived out their
lives in the weakness which depends on God as the giver, the
Corinthians spoke as men who were under obligation to no one.
Paul's severity, in his rebuke of the Corinthians, derived its
force from his own willingness to be addressed by the claims of
the cross, and by his willingness to allow that gospel to determine his vocation as an apostle. The first body-closing unit
is a manifestation of the nature of Paul's empowered speech; he
does not address the Corinthians from a vantage point of arbi-
trary power but in the manner of a father admonishing his child
("I do not write this to make you ashamed, but to admonish you
as my beloved children."). Paul's appeal is further strengthened
in 4:16, the second body-closing unit, by his call to the Corinthians to imitate him. This appeal is Paul's basis of confidence
in the Word's success among the Corinthians, i.e., they, like
he, must live out their lives in the manner of the cross, an
utter foolishness to the perishing but an enabling power and the
basis of confidence to those who are being saved.

c. Implementation of the Apostolic *Parousia*

Though the third unit of the body-closing is probably the
most forceful expression of Paul's apostolicity in the body-
closing and worthy of much attention for that reason, I will not
attempt to review the various passages connected with this structural unit. My primary intent throughout this chapter has been
to identify the phraseology, transitional constructions, and
structural elements within the body. Since I can add nothing
materially to Robert Funk's analysis of this third body-closing
unit,[100] I refer the reader to his excellent study.

CHAPTER THREE

COMPARISON OF THE BODY OF THE LETTER IN PAUL AND THE PAPYRI

Introduction

This study may be concluded by repeating briefly the nature
of the similarities and differences between the letter-body in
Paul and in the non-literary papyri. Though comparisons were
made at a number of points within the preceding chapter, we may
now pull out the specific aspects of the study related to this
question. These points of similarity and dissimilarity will be
discussed, first, in terms of general observations and, secondly,
by means of an analysis of the individual body-sections in Paul
and the papyri. General observations, regarding likeness and
difference, constitute section A of the chapter, while the comparison of the body-opening, the body-middle, and the body-
closing is, respectively, B, C, and D.

A. General Observations

1. *Similarities*

The body of the letter, both in the common Greek letter and
in Paul, divides into three structural components, designated,
respectively, body-opening, body-middle, and body-closing. The
point of transition at which each of these three sections begins,
both in Paul and in the papyri, is commonly marked by a formulaic or quasi-formulaic construction. Some of these stereotyped constructions are employed in more than one body-section,
and may be appropriately designated "general" transitional constructions. Not only do we find the analogous use of such constructions in Paul and the private Greek letter, we also find
that a few of the same constructions, e.g., the vocative and
the disclosure formula, are employed in both. Other stereotyped
constructions are confined largely to *one* body-section, and may
be appropriately called "specific" transitional constructions.
This state of affairs *also* holds for both Paul and the papyri.
And *all* of the "specific" body-opening formulae, as well as most
of the body-closing formulae, which we find in Paul, find their
parallel in the non-literary papyri.

93

In addition to these more technical or formal similarities, the "idea" (or "function") of the Pauline letter-body corresponds roughly to that of the common letter tradition. The body of the letter, in both Paul and the private Greek letter, is the "message" part of the letter, containing the primary information which the addressor wishes to convey.

2. *Differences*

The principal difference between the body of the Pauline letter and that of the private Greek letter is length. All three body-sections tend to be more extensive in Paul than in the papyri. Another difference, which is something of a corollary, is the introduction of additional subdivisions within two of the body-sections of the Pauline body. Whereas the body-middle is a rather amorphous entity in the papyri, it is constructed as two discrete parts in Paul. And, whereas the body-closing in the papyri may reproduce the principal occasion for writing (the motivation for writing formula) *and* urge action commensurate with this reason for writing (the responsibility formula), Paul adds a third structural element (the "confidence" formula) whereby he alleges confidence in the fulfillment of the request(s) made in his reiteration of the reason for writing. We shall take up these additions in more detail in the individual analysis of the body-middle and the body-closing.

Though the majority of the body-opening and the body-closing formulae in Paul have a counterpart in the papyri, few of his body-middle constructions find their parallel in the common letter tradition. Whereas the same transitional constructions occur from letter to letter in the body-middle of the common letter, largely unaffected by the particular message of the body, the major body-middle transitions in Paul are tailor-made to fit the message of the individual letter.

Even the "specific" body-opening and body-closing formulae in Paul, comments on the similarity of such formulae in Paul and the papyri notwithstanding, receive a form the phraseology of which slightly varies from comparable formulae in the common letter tradition.

B.   The Body-Opening

1. *Similarities*

Six different body-opening formulae are employed in the
seven Pauline letters of this study, and each one finds its parallel in the body-opening of the common Greek letter.[1]   Of
these six body-opening formulae, Paul, also like the papyri, employs the fuller form (i) of the disclosure formula much more
often than he does the other body-opening formulae.[2]

The body-opening also appears to perform the same function
in these seven Pauline letter bodies as it does in the private
Greek letter.   Whereas the general function of the body is to
impart information to someone at a distance, the body-opening
performs the specific role of introducing this information. The
body-opening introduces the information in such a way, either by
disclosing new information or by recalling previous communication of which both parties are cognizant, that a basis of mutu
ality is founded.   Once this matter of mutual concern has been
introduced, the body-middle may carry the relevant details forward.   This state of affairs exists both in Paul and in the private Greek letter.

2. *Dissimilarities*

Though analogous constructions in the papyri answer to each
of the body-opening formulae in Paul, Paul commonly takes liberties both with the form (the phraseology) and with the function
of these formulae.   The fuller form (i) of the disclosure formula, for example, has usually the following form in the papyri:
γινώσκειν σε θέλω ὅτι.., ("I want you to know that..."). The
corresponding form in Paul, however, is more often: οὐ θέλω
δὲ ὑμᾶς ἀγνοεῖν ὅτι...("I do not want you to be ignorant
that...").[3]

Similarly, Paul does not always follow the established patterns in the implementation of these formulae.   For example,
the expression of astonishment in Gal. 1:6, introduced by
θαυμάζω, functions differently in Paul than in the papyri. The
expression of astonishment in the body-opening of the papyri
functions, ordinarily, as the means whereby the addressor reproaches the addressee's failure to write.   This expression, in
turn, functions as the background of the request for a letter.

Though this expression is also an expression of dissatisfaction
and an intimation that communication has broken down in Galatians,
it does not function as the background of a request for a letter.
Paul's dissatisfaction is not the Galatians' failure to write but
their rejection of the gospel. Analogous liberties are taken in
Paul's use of the joy expression, the verb of hearing (ἀκούω),
and, on occasion, the fuller form (i) of the disclosure formula.[4]

The body-opening is considerably longer in the Pauline letters than in the papyri, and this length may account for the
larger number of formulae, which Paul employs (at least on one
occasion) in the body-opening. The maximum number of discrete
formulaic units, in the common letter tradition, seems to be two.
And, when the two body-opening formulae are employed, one (usually the first) functions as the background to the other, which is
most often a request. Though the maximum number of major body-
opening formulae is commonly two in Paul also, Paul employs four
discrete body-opening formulae in Galatians. Three of these four
formulae (the expression of astonishment in 1:6; the compliance
statement in 1:9; and the verb of hearing in 1:13) function as
the background to the disclosure formula in 1:11.

C. The Body-Middle

1. *Similarities*

The specific role which the body-middle of the private Greek
letter plays in the impartation of information is that of carrying forward the information introduced in the body-opening.
Either the relevant details of the message are developed; new,
and equally important matters of information, are introduced; or
new, but less important subjects, are presented. Similarly,
the body-middle of the Pauline letters functions as the means
whereby the information introduced in the body-opening is carried
forward. The information imparted in the body-opening is carried
forward, in each instance of the Pauline body-middle but Romans,
by the development of the relevant details of that message.

2. *Differences*

Though the purpose ("idea") of the body-middle is the same
in Paul and in the papyri, the manner of implementation varies
considerably. The body-middle of the private Greek letter tends

both to be more loosely structured, and more inconsistent in the
use of discrete formulae to indicate transitions, than either
the body-opening or the body-closing sections. Paul, on the
other hand, constructs the body-middle carefully and employs
discrete formulae at each of the major points of transition.

Paul constructs the body-middle, for example, as a two-membered entity (in every letter but Philem.). The first of these
two parts is always a tightly organized theological argument;
the second part, immediately following, is less tightly constructed, and is the place where the principles espoused in the
preceding part are concretized. The message introduced in the
body-opening, consequently, is developed according to its theoretical and practical aspects, respectively.

And, Paul is more perspicuous in his use of formulae in the
body-middle, perhaps, than in either the body-opening or body-
closing. He creates transitional constructions which are expressive of, and interwoven integrally into, the theological
argument. The major body-middle formulae, as a consequence, do
not correspond from letter to letter. Nor do they have parallels in the principal body-middle conventions of the common letter tradition.

D. The Body-Closing

1. *Similarities*

The purpose of the body-closing of the private Greek letter,
after the information introduced in the body-opening has been
carried forward in the body-middle (either by the development of
its relevant details or by the introduction of new information),
is to repeat the occasion for writing and to lay the basis for
future correspondence.

These two functions are reflected in the four principal
formulae employed in the body-closing.[5] The fullest body-closing
section has, usually, no more than three of these four formulae,
and the usual order is: (1) motivation for writing form (iii)
of the disclosure formula; (2) responsibility phrase (or courtesy request for a letter); and (3) reference to a coming visit.
The motivation for writing formula which introduces the body-
opening, by repeating the reason for writing, performs the first
of the two body-closing functions. And, this formula finalizes

the message of the body thereby, when the addressor's only desire is the disclosure of information. On the other hand, if the addressor expects some response to the information imparted, or if he has made an explicit request, one or more of the three remaining formulae may be employed subsequently. These formulae, in turn, are tied to the second function of the body-closing, i.e., the addressor's expectation establishes the basis for future correspondence.

The addressor employs, most often, one of the "responsibility" phrases, when he anticipates a response. These phrases, depending on the particular one employed, may promise benefit, be relatively neutral in intent, or threaten the addressee.

Another body-closing convention, related to the addressor's expectation, is the "courtesy request for a letter." The request, in these instances, is from the inferior to the superior in the epistolary situation. The addressor entreats the addressee to write for whatever he needs, in exchange for the favor which he himself asked previously.

The fourth formula, the addressor's desire or promise to visit, is usually the last element in the body-closing. The reference to a coming visit may be either separate from or related to the other body-closing formulae. If the formula is related to the other body-closing conventions in the letter, however, the anticipated visit carries either a nuance of threat or benefit. The visit should be construed, in either case, as the means of empowering the relationship already latent in the correspondence.

The function of the body-closing in the Pauline letters corresponds to what has been outlined here in relation to the body-closing of the common Greek letter. Even the implementation of the body-closing in Paul parallels, roughly, what we find in the papyri. Though the form (the "phraseology") is not identical, the intent and sequence of the formulae are quite similar. The body closing is introduced uniformly, for example, by a surrogate motivation for writing formula.[6] Similarly, the body-closing is concluded in the Pauline letters by Paul's reference to an anticipated visit--either that of himself or of an apostolic emissary. And, once again like the common letter tradition, the nature of the visit may be determined largely on the basis of the tenor of the preceding elements in the body-closing.

2. *Differences*

The greatest formal difference between the body-closing in
Paul and the corresponding section in the papyri is Paul's use
of a "confidence" formula, a formula which has no parallel in
the papyri. This formula's role in the body-closing may be
explicated in relation to its position. And, for the sake of
comparison, we may diagram, in order, the fullest form of the
body-closing in Paul and in the common letter tradition.

	the papyri		*Paul*
(i)	motivation for writing	(i)	motiv. for writing-responsibility phrase
(ii)	responsibility phrase	(ii)	confidence formula
(iii)	anticipated visit	(iii)	apostolic *parousia*

The confidence formula is Paul's means of alleging confidence
in the fulfillment of the claims set forth in the motivation for
writing-responsibility formula. The apostolic *parousia* convention, in turn, is a further means of empowering or actualizing
the expectations set forth in the motivation for writing formula.

Two other aspects of the dissimilarity of the Pauline body-
closing should not be overlooked. For example, whereas the
statement of an anticipated visit is relatively rare in the common letter tradition, the apostolic *parousia* is a regular item
in the Pauline body-closing. The letter was obviously a poor
substitute, in Paul's opinion, for his actual presence. Paul,
again unlike the common letter tradition, does not restate the
occasion for writing (the motivation for writing convention)
neutrally. The information which he has imparted, always connotes something--whether good or ill--regarding Paul's relation
to the congregation to which he writes.

Paul, as suggested above, also takes liberties with the form
(the phraseology) of each of the corresponding body-closing formulae. But since such details were treated in the preceding
chapter, it seems sufficient at this point, merely to recall
that such differences exist.

1. *The Form of the Ancient Greek Letter: A Study in Greek Epistolography* (Ph.D. dissertation, Catholic University of America, 1923).

2. "A" stands for the writer or addressor, "B" for the addressee. The former formula is used in all sorts of letters: private letters, business letters, communications between officials, as well as in letters from or to officials (cf. Exler, pp. 23-68). The latter is used in applications of various kinds: for rental or purchase, for notices in applications of various kinds: for rental or purchase, for notices of birth or death, for census and other official registrations, for complaints about injuries received, with a request for redress, etc.

3. The former characterizes familiar letters; the latter, petitions and formal complaints. Business letters generally omit the salutation entirely. διευτύχει began to replace εὐτύχει in the first century A.D.

4. "Studien zur Idee und Phraseologie des griechischen Briefes bis 400 n. Chr." *Annales Academiae Scientiarum Fennicae* (Sarja-Ser.B.Nede-Tom. 102,2), Helsinki, 1956. Koskenniemi's analysis discloses that a health wish was in common use throughout the Ptolemaic and Roman periods. It was originally a two-membered formula following the salutation: εἰ ἔρρωσαι (or ὑγιαίνεις), εὖ ἂν ἔχοι, καὶ αὐτὸς δ' ὑγίαινον. (If you are well, it would be excellent, I myself am well.") Later a shortened form of the health wish was used in which only the first member was retained, e.g., ὁ δεῖνα τῷ δεῖνι χαίρειν καὶ ἐρρῶσθαι. This form combined syntactically with the salutation. A new form of the formula had emerged by the second century: πρὸ (μὲν) πάντων (or πρὸ τῶν ὅλων) εὔχομαί σε ὑγιαίνειν (or ὁλοκληρεῖν). The formula in common use during the third and fourth centuries was: πρὸ μὲν πάντων εὔχομαι followed by a prayer that the writer might be privileged to meet the other again in good health: ...σε ὁλόκληρον ἀπολαβεῖν (or ...ὅπως ὁλόκληρόν σε ἀπόλαβω). The health wish was also used in the closing, immediately preceding the farewell, but was not used frequently until the Roman period.

   The *proskynema*-formula was a phrase used by the addressor to allege that he had prayed on the addressee's behalf. It was attached frequently to the health formula. This formula originated in Egyptian religious practice, according to Koskenniemi (139ff.), and was associated with a particular god (especially Sarapis). It was taken over by the Greeks and tied to the health formula. It is not always clear whether the formula reflects a real act of prayer or is merely a convention.

   Koskenniemi (148ff.) suggests that the greeting formula had three forms: the writer greets the addressee; the writer greets others through the addressee; the writer conveys greetings from another party to the recipient. Exler's analysis of the ἀσπάζομαι formula, though he places it within the body and not in the opening, is quite helpful. He notes that this form of greeting is found ordinarily at the end of letters (as early as the first century B.C.), but that it was transposed from the end of the letter to the beginning from the second century on.

5. The body offers more variety because it is the means whereby the occasion for writing unfolds and is, therefore, necessarily more personal and less stereotyped.

6. The body-opening and the body-closing are analyzed prior to the body-middle because the last is more difficult to delineate. The prior description of the body-opening and the body-closing is one way of circumscribing the boundaries of the section between, i.e., the body-middle. The body-middle, and its points of transition, is more difficult to define for the following reasons. (1) The common Greek letter of the Ptolemaic and Roman periods is generally short, and frequently the body-opening dovetails immediately into the body-closing or the letter-closing, i.e., there is no occasion for positing a body-middle. (2) The body of the letter is so fluid, on other occasions, that it is difficult to separate the body-middle from either the body-opening or the body-closing. (3) The transitions to the body-opening and the body-closing tend uniformly to be major, whereas transitions in the body-middle may mark either a major movement to a new subject or a more minor development of the present subject. The unequal weight of body-middle transitions prohibits a simple definition of the body-middle.

7. The fuller disclosure formula, i.e., γινώσκειν σε θέλω ὅτι..., does not emerge until the Roman period according to the editor of letter 83 of P.Mert.II(p.116). He suggests that the formula was first used in P.Oxy.743,1.27,2 B.C. The formula above, employing the verb ἀγνοέω,is probably an early surrogate, i.e., it also calls some matter of information to the recipient's attention. Other examples of the ἀγνοέω formula are: P.S.I.488,1,258/7 B.C.; P.Mich. 57,1,248 B.C.; P.Tebt.314,3ff., ii A.D.

8. Both the verbs γινώσκω and γνωρίζω may appear in the imperative form of the disclosure formula. I am not able to distinguish at this point any difference in nuance or difference in chronology between the two verbs.

9. Other examples of the imperative form: P.Mich.28,6f., 256 B.C.; P.S.I.56,5,ii B.C., etc.

10. Scores of examples of this form of the disclosure formula may be found and it is unnecessary, therefore, to add any more.

11. Most examples of the "motivation for writing" formula in the opening are from the Ptolemaic period (cf.exx.13-14). Other examples are: P.Hib.81,2f.,238 B.C.; P.Fay.123,3ff., ca.100 A.D.; P.Beatty.Panop.1,col.i,3,296/7 A.D. (The motivation for writing formula, when in the body-opening, is in business letters or official correspondence.)

12. Cf. exx. 1, 5-12.

13. The fuller form (i) and the imperative form (ii) appear to perform the same function. The imperative form predominates in business letters, however, where the addressor need not be so polite (cf. exx. 2-4). The motivation for writing form (iii) is illustrated in exx. 13-22.

14. Cf. P.Mich.514,8, iii A.D. and P.Tebt.408,3ff., 3 A.D.
    (these letters are not listed above).

15. This formula is more characteristic of the body-closing
    (cf. exx. 16-22) than the body-opening (exx. 13-15) since
    examples in the body-opening are usually confined to Ptol-
    emaic business letters.

16. This state of affairs is not surprising since the perfect
    indicative (iv) and the participial form (v) are commonly
    used for more minor transitions (cf. exx. 32-37) and one
    should expect minor transitions to appear more often in
    the body-middle than major. The participial form, both in
    the body-middle and in the body-opening, forms a subordi-
    nate clause and cannot have, therefore, independent transi-
    tional value. The common function of the participial form
    of the disclosure formula is to provide a "background" to
    the principal clause of the sentence within which it occurs.
    (The classical form of the "background" is found in the
    letter of petition [cf. the author's M.A. thesis: *The Form
    and Structure of the Official Petition*, SBL Dissertation
    Series 5, Missoula, Montana, 1972]which uniformly has a
    background section preceding the actual statement of re-
    quest. This background section delineated the circumstance
    [s] necessitating the request. The background [or the oc-
    casion] for the request does not always precede the request,
    however, in private letters. When it precedes it is usual-
    ly introduced by an ἐπεί [or ἐπειδή] clause. And when it
    appears to be omitted, the subject matter that had to be
    delineated in the background is often expressed subsequent-
    ly by ἵνα, ὅπως, or γάρ clauses. The participial form of
    the disclosure formula [v] may also function as the back-
    ground to a request. In addition, it often acts as a
    background to other kinds of constructions.)

17. Cf. exx. 5 and 6 (2 exx. out of the 12).

18. Cf. exx. 7-12 (one-half of the 12 total references).

19. Very few examples of the μὴ ἀμελήσῃς phrase occur before
    the second century A.D.; from that time on it is found fre-
    quently (cf. R. C. Horn, *The Use of the Subjunctive and
    Optative Moods in the Non-Literary Papyri*, Philadelphia,
    1926, 94). He notes (96) that this phrase is found only
    in I Tim. 4:14 in the New Testament.

20. This phrase (μὴ ἄλλως ποιήσῃς) is common only in the third
    century B.C. and the first and second A.D. (cf. Horn, 96).

21. The verb ἐπιμελέομαι recurs intermittently in responsibility
    phrases throughout the body but is found most often in the
    body-closing. A partial explanation for the larger number
    there may lie in the use of a short exhortation to the re-
    cipient to take care of his health in the letter-closing.
    This exhortation, constructed with a form of the verb
    ἐπιμελέομαι (cf. Koskenniemi, 133f.) may have suggested
    the use of ἐπιμελέομαι in the body-closing, either as an
    independent formula or as a means of syntactically combin-
    ing the body-closing and letter-closing.

22. All four items are found in exx. 2, 3, and 6 (we find a
    surrogate for item (i) in ex. 2 and a surrogate for item
    (iv) in ex. 3). Four of the remaining five examples,
    exx. 1, 4, 5, and 7, have three of the four items (exx. 1,

4, and 5 omit only the last item, the adv. denoting the degree of grief; ex. 7 omits the first item). The remaining example, (8), has items (ii) and (iii).

23. John Winter, *Life and Letters in the Papyri* (Ann Arbor: University of Michigan Press, 1933).

24. The other verb meaning "to send" (πέμπω) is found more often in the Roman period than in the Ptolemaic (cf. exx. 4-5, 9, 12-13).

25. The first example in the body-closing above, ex. 8 (regarding the sending of oil-makers), seems to be an afterthought. Similar examples in the body-closing, not listed, are: P.Mich.217,16ff., 296 A.D.; P.S.I.395,6f., 241/40 B.C.

26. Horn (38) suggests that this form of the condition is the most frequent. My own analysis confirms his suggestion. A number of set phrases employing ἐάν and the subjunctive appear, on initial examination, to be clichés, but Horn suggests (38ff.) that specific phrases recur in certain kinds of letters, e.g., ἐὰν οὖν σοι φαίνηται in appeals, petitions, and the like. The frequent use of stereotyped protases in certain letter types indicates, therefore, that they are something of a structural item. (My own analysis of such phrases in petitions [White, *The Form and Structure of Official Petitions*, 43, 48ff.] has led me to accept Mullin's ["Petition as a Literary Form," *Novum Testamentum*, V (January, 1962), 46-54] terminology for them: "elaborations." He calls them "elaborations" because they are not actually essential to the structure of the petition. They embellish or buttress structural items, however, and are a means of making a more compelling entrée to the recipient. These phrases, therefore, are not merely ornamental.)

The following examples illustrate the stereotyped phraseology which appears in certain kinds of documents. We find the following conditional phrases in requests and petitions: ἐὰν φαίνηται ("if you approve"), from the iii B.C. to the early iv A.D.; ἐὰν δόξῃς ("if you approve"), primarily in the Roman period; εἰ δοκεῖ, frequently in the iii B.C.; εἰ δόξῃ in the late Byzantine period; and ἐὰν ᾖ ταῦτα ἀληθῆ ("if these things are true"), in the Ptolemaic period. The following are characteristic of wills and/or marriage contracts: ἐὰν δέ τι ἀνθρώπινον πάθω, most frequent in the Ptolemaic period; ἐὰν τελευτήσω, in the Roman period. Other set phrases, and the documents in which they may be found, are analyzed by Horn on 38ff.

All the set phrases noted here (and the majority of those analyzed by Horn) are characteristic of official documents. They are not immediately relevant, therefore, to the study at hand.

27. The condition may function either positively, by promising benefits to the addressee should he do what the addressor wants (cf. the subsequent analysis of conditions in the body-closing since no exx. of the positive form are listed above), or negatively, by threatening the addressee should he be negligent (cf. exx. 3-8). The use of the condition for a threat is an established usage. Classical Greek emplaoyed εἰ and the future indicative, for example, to imply

a veiled threat. The subjunctive with ἐάν is also used to imply a threat in the non-literary papyri. The condition is not the only stereotyped means for making a threat, however, in the papyri (cf. the subsequent analysis of the body-closing).

28. "Petitions," written pleas for redress addressed to public officials, uniformly contain two major body sections: "background" and "request period." The background (cf. n. 16 for a fuller explanation of background) delineates the circumstances necessitating the request while the request period specifies what is requested and the anticipated justice the petitioner will receive if the request is granted. The vocative is a discrete item within the request, e.g., δέομαι οὖν σου, βασιλεῦ, εἴ σοι δοκεῖ,...("I entreat you therefore, king, if you approve,..."),ex.9.

29. These letter-opening conventions were delineated on p. 1. The health wish and prayer formula were explicated in some detail in n. 4.

30. The letter-opening and the body-opening are obviously not separated as I have illustrated them (either here or on p.18. They have been separated to facilitate the reader's identification (the solid line separates the letter opening and the body-opening).

31. Other complaints about failure to write may be found in Winter, 83ff. and Koskenniemi, 64ff. Koskenniemi suggests that in the Ptolemaic period these complaints were limited to cases where definite news was expected. Complaints became more generalized and frequent, however, by the Roman period. We may note, as Koskenniemi suggests (64ff.) that in addition to the verb θαυμάζω, (found in the introductory example of this section), two other words often signal disappointment over the disruption of the epistolary relationship: ἤδη (exx. 3 and 5), ἰδού (ex. 6). Koskenniemi suggests that complaints regarding failure to write were not typical. The epistolary situation was usually pleasant and a large number of requests for a letter, therefore, take the following form: γράφε δὲ καὶ σὺ ἡμῖν ὧν ἂν χρείαν ἔχῃς ("And you must write to us about anything you require."), followed by a request for something concrete. This formula is usually in the body-closing (cf. the subsequent analysis of the body-closing).

32. This third element is either (a) or (b) but not both.

33. The entire body of some letters revolves around such requests. Further investigation may reveal the emergence of the request for a visit as a discrete letter-type. Another formulaic request opening the body is the notification of safe arrival or extended stay at a foreign port (cf. P.Cairo Zen.59251,2ff., 252 B.C.; P.Oxy.744,3ff., 1 B.C.; B.G.U.423,6ff., ii A.D.; and Class.Phil.xxii.p.243, 4ff., ii A.D.). The sole purpose of letters whose bodies open with a statement concerning either arrival or extended stay is, in many cases, to relieve worry about the addressor's welfare. The notifications sometimes function also as the background to the request for a letter. The purpose of the return letter, it seems, was to relieve the addressor's own concern for the other's welfare.

34. Item (3) is not actually illustrated in the examples. The material under item (3) in the diagram, therefore, is from an unquoted segment of the body.

35. "Studien zur Idee und Phraseologie," 75ff. (cf. the examples listed by Koskenniemi).
    I have discerned four alternative patterns. Items within these formulae, but not necessarily in the same sequence, are as follows:
    (a) a statement regarding the arrival of a letter + the verb χαίρω in the first person of the aorist tense + an adverb (λίαν, μεγάλως, πολλά, etc.) expressing the magnitude of the joy + the occasion for the joy denoted by various means, i.e. introduced by ὅτι, ὡς, διά with the accusative, the participle, ἐπί, or πῶς, (cf. exx.1 and 6).
    (b) a statement regarding the arrival of a letter + the noun χάρις in the accusative + the verb ἔχω in the first person indicative + an adverb of magnitude + the object of the joy denoted by various means (ex.4).
    (c) a verb of hearing or learning + the object of what was heard or learned denoted by ὅτι + the verb χαίρω in the first person of the aorist tense + an adverb expressing magnitude (exx. 3 and 5).
    (d) a formula with items corresponding to (a) except the phrase εὐχαρίστω τοῖς θεοῖς functions as a surrogate for the verb χαίρω (ex. 2).
    Pattern (a) is the form of the joy expression most often encountered. On the basis of my analysis, it is found as often as the other three forms combined.

36. The following items are commonly found in compliance formulae: (1) an introductory adverb (καθώς, καθότι, or ὡς) + (2) the verb ἐντέλλω (in a past tense; either: "I instructed you" or "You instructed me") + (3) the object of the instruction denoted by περί + (4) a statement concerning either the fulfillment of the instruction or an assertion regarding the addressor's confidence in the addressee's fulfillment.

37. The frequent intertwining aspect of these two body-closing features may be explicated as follows. The body-closing not only reiterates the principal motivation for writing but connotes simultaneously (in many cases) the nature of the relationship between the two parties in the epistolary situation. The nature of that relationship--whether good or bad--and the emphatic reiteration of the purpose for writing function in tandem as the basis on which future communication is built.

38. θαυμάζω is usually employed in the body-opening as one of the items of formulaic complaints regarding failure to write (pp. 19-21). It sometimes functions (as here), however, with other nuances in the body-opening. In all the examples which I have examined, whatever the nature of the nuance, the expression of astonishment is one of dissatisfaction.

39. These two types were: disclosure formulae and responsibility statements. A third type of formula, reassurances, was also analyzed, but since they are infrequent in the body-closing they are not included.

40. The abbreviation, ἵνα εἰδῆς, both in letter (4) and elsewhere demonstrates the established nature of the formula. Further examples may be found in Koskenniemi, 77ff.

41. Mayser (*Grammatik*, ii.I,p.283) notes that the use of εἰ
    with the future indicative in the papyri often, as in class-
    ical Greek, implies a veiled threat. Most examples of εἰ
    with the future, however, are found in the Ptolemaic period.
    ʼEάν with the subjunctive is also used, during the Roman
    period, for a veiled threat. The following letters con-
    tain the threat clause stated in the form of a condition:
    P.Hib.42,8ff.,262/61 B.C.; P.Mich.72,17ff.,*ca*.mid.iii B.C.;
    P.Mich.21,7f.,257 B.C.; P.Tebt.767,11ff., ii B.C.; P.Mert.
    80,11ff., ii A.D.; P.Fay.124,19ff., ii A.D.; P.Beatty Panop.
    2,col.ix,219,300 A.D.; P.Mert.29,6ff., iii/iv A.D.,etc.

42. This formula is frequent in "Letters of Recommendation,"
    following the addressor's request (as here, in ex.1), but
    it also appears in other letters (also following a request,
    exx. 2-4).

43. See the previous analysis of "Complaints about Failure to
    Write" in the body-opening (19-21 and n. 31). See Kosken-
    niemi's analysis of these courtesy requests for a letter
    (67-73).

44. Koskenniemi reviews the scholarly theory regarding the na-
    ture of the Greek letter (*die Lehre*, "The Theory": 18-63).
    The letter, according to the theory, is the following:
    (1) a demonstration of friendship, *philophronesis*; (2) a
    mode of spiritual presence in a time of bodily absence,
    parousia; (3) a conversation, in the sense of an intimate
    personal relationship, *homilia*. The major portion of
    Koskenniemi's study, however, is an analysis of the nature
    of the Greek letter as revealed by the letters themselves
    (*die Praxis*, "The Practice": 64-200). The major function,
    as it emerges from actual letters, is that of continuing
    an interpersonal relationship. The theory and the practice
    are one since both suggest that the letter should be com-
    pared to a conversation and functions as a continuing con-
    tact between men.
        Winter suggests a similar function for letters by
    citing, approvingly, Libanius' definition: "A letter is
    a meeting in writing which satisfies a necessary purpose
    between two persons who are separated. In it one speaks
    as if face to face with the one who is absent" (85). McFee
    (*Letters from an Ocean Tramp*, 57) says: "A letter is some-
    thing which would not be set down if the two persons con-
    cerned were within speaking distance."

45. Many of the references to an anticipated visit, due to the
    unclear nature of the epistolary situation (or simply be-
    cause the addressor did not intend that the visit have
    either an especially menacing or beneficial quality), appear
    neutral in intent.

46. See n.6 and the reasons adduced there for the difficulty
    in analyzing the middle of the body.

47. Both are employed either to signal the movement to a new
    and important subject or to call attention to some aspect
    of major importance in the material already presented.
    The fuller form is identified as a major transition even
    more readily if the vocative is included in the formula.
    The imperative form, as elsewhere within the body, usually
    appears in business letters as the less polite surrogate
    for the full form. The full form is employed in private
    correspondence other than business letters.

48. A certain negative value is probably implied, however, by the very paucity of examples.

49. These reassurances are primarily of two types: reassurances regarding the addressor's health and reassurances regarding the performance of some task or responsibility.

    The characteristic body-middle constructions are probably a legitimate index for determining the nature of the body-middle, although, at this point, I am unable to suggest either a coherent systematization of transitional constructions or a meaningful interpretation of their function. This means, of course, that subsequent remarks are more of a descriptive nature than interpretive. The present state of affairs does not deny, necessarily, the validity of employing the body-middle constructions for such an index--especially since a similar procedure proved helpful in interpreting the body-opening and body-closing. The author only confesses that, at this stage of the investigation, he has not been able to use these constructions for such criteria.

50. This use of ὅτι to introduce direct discourse is frequent in papyri letters and especially prevalent in references to writing.

51. Καλῶς (or εὖ) ποιήσεις is the usual means for introducing requests in private letters. These formulaic words are, according to Koskenniemi (134), a "common, polite circumlocution for the imperative." The request proper that follows is, as here, often in the aorist participle form. The verb "to write" is not the only verb employing this convention, but the concatenation formed by this verb and the convention is so frequent, in the body-middle, that it warrants recognition as a specific body-middle formula.

52. The two formulaic features of (b) are: (1) the aor. act. imperative form of the verb γράφω; (2) explicit reference to the recipient of the letter (the unemphatic form of the personal pronoun in the dative case), immediately following the command to write.

53. These aspects of the verb may cause one to question its identification as a formula. The following features of the verb of saying, however, have led me to suggest that it is a specific body-middle formula: the verb λέγω, apart from the verb meaning "to know" probably occurs more often than any other verb of saying or thinking in the body; λέγω seems to have a special affinity with the body-middle; it is conceivable, in light of these aspects, that λέγω is employed in a *number* of formulaic ways which, at this point, the analyst is not able to reduce to paradigms.

54. Verbs of saying have one noticeable formulaic feature: the preference for the conjunction δέ. This fact is interesting in view of the fact that the verb of informing formulae regularly prefers the conjunction καί.

55. Receipt-transfer statements (pp.10-12), have a special affinity with the body-middle, whereas περί with the genitive (16f.) and the vocative (15f.) are just as common elsewhere. Receipt-transfer statements and the vocative commonly signal points of major transition. Περί with the genitive, on the other hand, may function for either major or minor transitions.

56. The vocative often combines syntactically with a formulaic phrase (especially the fuller (i) disclosure formula), but it seems to indicate a major transition point even when it does not accompany a formula.

57. These first three categories are "general", i.e., they may be found in other parts of the body (the third category, reassurances, could probably be considered "specific" since it is more characteristic of the body-middle than of the other two body parts). Two other "general" formulae, grief expressions and responsibility statements, sometimes appear in the body-middle but their number is negligible and, therefore, are not included.

58. I depend on Koskenniemi (pp.91-95) for the conception that the two tasks of the letter are the imparting of information and the maintenance of personal contact. I have extended his suggestions, however, through the recognition that the opening and closing letter parts are the principal agents for the latter task (i.e., the maintenance of personal contact), while the body is the primary means of expressing the former (i.e., imparting information). The extension is legitimate because, in my opinion, it is implicit in Koskenniemi's analysis of the "forms of address" (pp.95-104) that open the letter and in his comments on "family letters" (104-14). This suggestion may be illustrated by reference to his section on "family letters." The primary concern of most family letters, he suggests, is the maintenance of family ties, not the impartation of information. They tend to be formal, monotonous, and lacking in creativity. They fail, according to Koskenniemi, to utilize the possibilities the letter provides. Implicit in his suggestion that family letters fail to utilize the possibilities of the letter is the notion that they are merely extended greetings (letter-opening) and that they contain no actual body ("message").

59. The opening statement of the body is the matter which the *addressor* considers the greatest mutual concern. This does not mean, of course, that the addressee considers the matter of equal import.

60. The body-opening follows immediately upon the cessation of the letter opening parts (i.e., the salutation, greetings, health-wish, and *proskynema* formula) and usually introduces the principal motivation for writing. The body-closing immediately precedes the letter closing conventions (i.e., health-wish, closing greetings, and the farewell proper) and commonly reiterates the principal motivation(s) for writing.

61. It may, for example, introduce a new subject matter of major import or it may fill in details of the opening subject that are of minor import. The body-middle, also unlike opening or closing, often contains more than one point of transition. If the transition is major, however, it is usually marked by formulaic phraseology.

1.   A.Deissmann, *Bible Studies,* A. Grieve, trans. (Edinburgh:
      T & T Clark, 1901), 3-59.

2.   The inaccuracy of the former suggestion above (i.e., that
      the letter has no fixed form) was demonstrated, in relation
      to the common letter tradition, in my analysis of the let-
      ter-body of the private Greek letter. Subsequent comments
      below, on the Pauline studies since Deissmann (as well as
      my own later analysis of the Pauline letter-body) will in-
      dicate that Deissmann was also wrong about the Pauline let-
      ter. The inappropriateness of the latter (i.e., that one
      may understand the Pauline letter by means of the common
      letter tradition) has been demonstrated (cf. subsequent
      comments below), in bits and pieces, by those interpreters
      who find parallels to discrete sections of Paul's letters
      in traditions other than that of the letter.

3.   Robert W. Funk, "The Letter: Form and Style," *Language,*
      Hermeneutic, and Word of God (New York: Harper and Row,
      1966), 250-274.

4.   P. Wendland, "Die urchristlichen Literaturformen," im
      Handbuch zum Neuen Testament I,3 (Tübingen: J.C.B. Mohr
      [Paul Siebeck], 1912), 339-45.

5.   Dibelius identified paraenesis first in James 1,3:13ff.,4,
      and 5 (*Der Brief des Jakobus,* herausgegeben und erganzt
      von Heinrich Greeven, *Meyers Kommentar* XV [11th ed.; Göt-
      tingen: Vandenhoeck & Ruprecht, 1964], 15f.), where he
      found general moral maxims strung together without refer-
      ence to a particular situation. The closest parallels to
      the style of James in the New Testament, he suggested,
      are certain sections in the Pauline letters (15). Cf.
      Funk's review of the studies on paraenesis (254-256).

6.   P. Schubert, *Form and Function of the Pauline Thanksgivings,*
      Beihefte *ZNW* 20 (Berlin: Töpelmann, 1939). Schubert found
      that the thanksgiving periods fall into two discrete types,
      which are occasionally mixed (35f.).

7.   J. Robinson, "Die Hodajot-Formel in Gebet und Hymnus des
      Fruhchristentums," in *Apophoreta. Festschrift für Ernst*
      Haenchen, W. Eltester, ed. (Berlin: Töpelmann, 1964),
      194-235. Whereas Schubert demonstrated that the thanks-
      givings reflect Hellenistic epistolary style (e.g., the
      proskynema formula), Robinson contends that they also were
      dependent on primitive Christian liturgical style. The
      two thanksgiving types (designated "Ia" and "Ib"), identi-
      fied by Schubert, correspond, according to Robinson, to
      the *hodaya* and *beracha* respectively.

8.   J. Sanders, "The Transition from Opening Epistolary Thanks-
      giving to Body in the Letters of the Pauline Corpus," *JBL*
      81 (1962), 348-62.

9.   Robert Funk, "The Apostolic *Parousia*: Form and Significance,"
      in *Christian History and Interpretation:* Studies Presented
      to John Knox, ed. W. R. Farmer, C. F. D. Moule, R. R. Nie-
      buhr (Cambridge: University Press, 1967), 249-268. Funk's
      nomenclature is derived from the fact that the various
      aspects of Paul's apostolic "presence" converge in this

one section of the body. The three different but related aspects of his presence are: the aspect of the letter; the apostolic emissary; and his own personal presence.

10. R. Bultmann, *Exegetische Probleme des zweiten Korintherbriefes,* "Symbolae Biblicae Upsalienses," Supplementhäfaten till Svensk Exegetisk Arsbok 9 (Uppsala, 1947; reprinted Darmstadt: Wissenschaftliche Buchgesellschaft, 1963).

11. Cf. the preceding analysis of the respective body-sections, and the characteristic phraseology employed to open each of these major points of transition, in ch. I.

12. Rudolf Bultmann suggested that the dialogical elements in Paul's letters were related to the popular and oral philosophy of the day, exemplified preeminently in the Cynic-Stoic *diatribe (Der Stil der paulinischen Predigt und die kynischstoische Diatribe,* "Forschungen zur Religion und Literature des Alten und Neuen Testaments," 13 (Göttingen: Vandenhoeck & Ruprecht, 1910). This style may also reflect Semitic influence, according to Bultmann, but he chose to deal only with the Greek *diatribe.* Hartwig Thyen, a pupil of Bultmann, extended his teacher's work by examining the Jewish background of the dialogical elements, particularly the investigation of the Jewish-Hellenistic homily (*Der Stil der Judisch-Hellenistischen Homilie,*"Forschungen zur Religion und Literature des Alten und Neuen Testaments," 47 (Göttingen: Vandenhoeck & Ruprecht, 1955). I suggest that Paul's dialogical style, though probably dependent on both the Hellenistic *diatribe* and the Jewish-Christian homily, is largely confined to the second major segment of the bodymiddle described above. (cf. the other sections of the Pauline letter [e.g., the thanksgiving, cf. n.7; paraenesis, cf. n.5] which draw on a nonepistolary tradition). The demonstration of the dialogical characteristics of the second major body-middle section will be presented subsequently (54, 56, 58).

13. Paul Schubert contributed materially to the delineation of the body-opening of the Pauline letter by his form-critical analysis of the thanksgiving period (cf.n.6). He observed that the thanksgiving period regularly followed upon the salutation (in all Pauline letters except Galatians) and *immediately preceded* the opening of the body. The opening of the body is established, consequently, by determining the close of the thanksgiving period. We cannot rely entirely on Schubert's analysis, however, as a means of identifying the body-opening, primarily for two reasons: (1) Though it is almost impossible to miss the opening of the thanksgiving, it is not so easy to determine where the thanksgivings terminate. (2) Since Galatians does not have a thanksgiving, we must employ other criteria there in order to establish the body-opening. Jack T. Sanders (n.8) extended Schubert's analysis of the thanksgiving period, especially in respect to the point of termination (Schubert delineated the close primarily in respect to those thanksgivings which reached an "eschatological climax": I Cor., Phil., II Thess.), and has proceeded to analyze the formula employed to introduce the body of the letter. This same formula (though sometimes slightly modified), he notes, is also utilized within the body to mark a transition in the argument or to introduce a new topic. His analysis,

though substantively sound, is subject to correction. The formula which he identifies formally, as rightly suggested, is employed elsewhere within the body and corresponds to that body of formulae designated "general" (i.e., common to more than one body-part) in this study. He takes what are two discrete formulae in the papyri (the "request" formula and the "disclosure" formula), however, and collapses them into one form. Taking the typical body-opening formulae of the papyri as a point of departure, we are also in a position to identify four additional body-opening formulae in Philemon, Galatians, and Romans (identified subsequently, 48ff.).

14. The form of the joy expression in Philem. 7 is: χαρὰν γὰρ πολλὴν ἔσχον καὶ παράκλησιν ἐπὶ τῇ ἀγάπῃ σου, ὅτι τὰ σπλάγχνα τῶν ἁγίων ἀναπέπαυται διὰ σοῦ, ἀδελφέ. ("For I have derived much joy and comfort from your love, my brother, because the hearts of the saints have been refreshed through you.") This form of the joy expression corresponds to that designated "b" in ch. I (cf. ex. 4 on p.23). Items within "b" were: (1) a statement regarding the arrival of a letter; (2) the noun χάρις in the acc.; (3) the vb. ἔχω in the first person indicative; (4) an adv. of magnitude; (5) the object of joy denoted by various means (ὅτι, ὡς, διά with the acc., the ptcp., ἐπί or πῶς).Only the first item of this form, i.e., the statement regarding the arrival of a letter, is missing in Philemon.

The major force of the formula in Philemon is accentuated by the presence of the vocative, ἀδελφε, which is employed also at points of major transition within the letter-body.

15. There is some question regarding what Paul actually requests. The matter turns on the force of the preposition περί in the appeal παρακαλῶ σε περὶ τοῦ ἐμοῦ τέκνου (v.10). John Knox (*Philemon Among the Letters of Paul* [rev. ed.; Nashville and New York: Abingdon Press, 1959], 22) phrases the issue as follows: "Is Paul appealing *on behalf of* Onesimus? Or is he simply asking *for* Onesimus?"

16. Cf. John White, *The Form and Structure of the Official Petition* (41ff.), for an analysis of the most common forms of the request period in the official petition. Not all the possible items found in the formal petition appear in Philem. 8ff., but the three items specified above are the only items regularly found in *private* Greek letters. The content of the request is usually not introduced by περί but by the ἵνα clause of purpose; for an example of περί employed for this purpose, however, see P.Oxy. 1070, 8ff., iii A.D.

17. These differences do not imply, necessarily, that Paul was dependent on a literary convention other than the private Greek letter. Both this example and the evidence of similar liberty in the form and use of the opening joy expression--as well as with opening formulae yet to be reviewed--suggest that Paul does not rigidly follow the established patterns. Paul's own creativity, working in conjunction with conditions prevailing in his ministry at the time and in relation to the established epistolary conventions, has determined the difference in form and function. An interpretation of the request in Philem. 8-14 that takes the

conditions under which the letter was written into account
as an explanation of its form is given by Knox (30ff.). Knox
suggests, for example, that the large and unusual request
which Paul makes (the request *for* Philemon) is the basis
from which we may understand the hesitation and indirection
of the request--as well as the measure of ambiguity at each
of the crucial points.

These innovations should cause us to be alert to the
flexibility with which Paul stands in relation to the letter
as a literary convention. We may anticipate, consequently,
modifications elsewhere in the body.

18. Cf. ch. I (19ff.). The expression is usually introduced
with θαυμάζω (in the first person) and is often accompanied
by the vocative or some other form of exclamatory address,
plus the object of astonishment introduced by ὅτι. The
vocative is absent in Gal. 1:6f.

19. Cf. ch. I, n.36. (1) The introductory adv., ὡς, above,
agrees with the customary form. (2) Though there is no precise parallel for προειρήκαμεν above, it is a recognizeable
substitute for the customary verb in the formula, ἐντέλλω
("I instructed"). Cf. also II John 4 and III John 3 (where
ἐχάρην λίαν, the opening joy expression, combines syntactically with a compliance form).

20. The reference is to something said previously in Galatia
not to what is written immediately preceding in v. 8. (cf.
Stamm, *The Interpreter's Bible,* 10 [Nashville: Abingdon
Press, 1953], 452 and Duncan, *Galatians* [*The Moffatt Com-
mentary*; New York: Harper & Brothers, 1935], 19, who also
suggest that it is better to take v. 9 as a reference to
previous communication in Galatia, but neither seize on
the importance of ὡς as a convention signalling previous
instruction).

21. Gal. 1:11f. and Rom. 1:13.

22. The verb ἀκούω in the body-opening is tied customarily to
an expression of grief or anxiety (cf. ch. I, 9f. and n.22).
The sequence and usual number of items in the formula are:
(1) the verb ἀκούω (or ἐπιγινώσκω) in the participial form;
(2) the object of the report stated by various constructions;
(3) the verb λυπέω *(or* ἀγωνιάω in the aorist active form)
in the aorist passive; (4) the adverb λίαν (or some other
surrogate denoting the degree of grief).

23. Cf. F. Blass and A. Debrunner, *A Greek Grammar of the New
Testament and Other Early Christian Literature,*Robert W.
Funk, trans. and rev. (Chicago: University of Chicago Press,
1961), sec. 477 (2).

24. The major import of 1:15 is signalled by the formulaic use
of ὅτε δέ to introduce the temporal clause. The same construction (ὅτε δέ) is employed at the next major point of
transition within the body-middle (cf. the subsequent discussion of this formula, 55).

25. The only example of the double negative which I found in
the papyri was P.Mich.6,1,257 B.C. But this form is found
elsewhere in Paul.

26. Cf. 31ff. concerning the major body-middle conventions.
Paul does not use (1) "responsibility" expressions, (2)
receipt-transfer statements, (3) formulaic references to
writing, and (4) the tandem conjunction δὲ καί (apart from

Philem. 22 and even there δὲ καί probably marks a transition
within the body-*closing*), unlike the papyri, as major transitional devices in the body-middle.

27. Paul also employs verbs of saying and the περί with the
genitive construction within the body-middle, but not with
the major transitional force they exert frequently in the
papyri. An important exception, however, is the major
transitional force of the verb of saying in the body-
middle of I Cor. 1:17-3:1 (cf. the subsequent analysis,
79f.).

28. Like so many of the private Greek letters, the body-middle
of Philemon is negligible. The body-middle at best extends
only from 15-18 and this section is neither opened nor
closed by formulae. The only transition within the segment which could be considered in any sense major is the
conditional sentence in 17, which, because the conjunction
οὖν and the imperative is employed, is probably the point
in the letter at which the resolution of the previous discussion is introduced. The body-middle is closed, consequently, in the following verse.

29. Cf. 46f.

30. The primary transitional device which Paul created for this
purpose in the body-middle of Galatians is a temporal construction, ὅτε δέ. The corresponding construction in the
letter to the Romans is οὐ γάρ. Other major formulae and
constructions play an important role, but, by and large,
they are either dependent on or inferior to these devices.

31. Paul demanded recognition of his apostleship (2:8) from
his congregation. Though this claim is not part of his
gospel, it bears on the question of its legitimacy. The
basis of his commission to apostleship was the revelation
of God's son (1:15f.), a commission from God transcending
even that of the "twelve," since it was a call to evangel-
ize the Gentiles (1:16; 2:2; 2:7ff.), i.e., Paul's gospel
came not from human ordination but from God himself.

32. Gal. 4:12-20 is provisionally excluded from the body-
middle section because, for reasons to be adduced subsequently, it should be analyzed in connection with the body-
closing.

33. These three clusters of formulae may be explicated in the
following manner. The first group emphasizes a point previously scored in relation to Paul himself and the gospel,
i.e., in order to be congruent with the nature of the gospel the Galatians' life must be one which is lived out of
faith by grace. The two formulae of the second cluster
deal with the relation between gospel and law. The purpose
of the final aggregate is to establish that those who live
their life out of faith by grace are the true inheritors
of the promise made to Abraham.

34. Part II of the body, as suggested earlier (p. 47 and n.12)
has affinities with the *diatribe*, which according to Bultmann (*Der Stil der paulinischen Predigt,* 10ff.), spins
itself out in the form of speech and rebuttal. The speaker
(or writer) indicates his contact with his audience by
various means; through challenges, rhetorical questions,
questions in rapid succession, imperatives, etc. The
practical segment of the body-middle of Galatians (represented by the 7 transitional phrases above) is congruent with
the style of the *diatribe*. The introductory formula in

this applicative segment, for example, is in the form of
a challenge (Gal.3:1); the second point of transition is
a rhetorical question (3:2); the third, an imperative (3:7);
the fourth, a question (3:19. This form of the question is
customary in the *diatribe*. This, and other similar little
questions [e.g., τί οὖν, τί γάρ, τί δέ, ποῦ οὖν], effect the
essential transitional points in the discussion and is the
means by which the speaker challenges himself and his hearers to reflect on the consequences which result therefrom.);
the fifth is a metaphorical comparison (Bultmann suggested
that metaphors were employed by the speaker in the *diatribe*
in such a way that the picture and the reality so merged
into one another that he addressed his hearers under the
title of the picture. Paul pictures the inheritor, who
is under age, as a slave in 4:1. Thereupon, the illustrated truth is related to the Galatians by the οὕτως clause
[a frequent device in the *diatribe*] in 4:3-5); and, finally,
the Galatians are addressed also under the form of a meta-
phor in the sixth and seventh transitions (4:28 and 4:31).

Attention should also be directed to the quasi formulaic role that λέγω performs in 3:15-4:31. The verb is
used a total of six times (3:15; 3:16; 3:17; 4:1; 4:21;
and 4:30). The difficulty in assigning a discrete transitional role to this verb, however, depends on two factors:
(1) other than the verb itself, no consistent phraseology
is employed; (2) the verb appears to be used in different
ways. With regard to the latter, on three occasions (3:16;
4:21; and 4:30) the verb introduces a scriptural proof-text
to support Paul's argument; on two occasions (3:17 and 4:1)
the verb is the equivalent of an explanatory clause; and
in the remaining reference (3:15) the verb introduces an
illustration drawn from everyday life to support Paul's
argument. The first and the third use may have a common
function, i.e., to introduce some type of illustration
which will support Paul's argument. We found an analogous
ambiguity in the use of λέγω in the body-middle of the
private Greek letter (p.35 exx. 5-8 on 35f., and n.54).

We also find the verb of saying employed in the *diatribe*, however (cf. Bultmann, 10, 13, 45, etc.), and Paul
is drawing on that tradition, perhaps, as much as on the
letter tradition.

35. The first section, 1:18-2:12, is "condemning" righteousness
which is introduced by οὐ γάρ in 1:16 (this οὐ γάρ also
introduces the theme for the entirety of Part I) and is
concluded by the same construction in 2:11. The second
section (2:13-3:22), "justifying" righteousness, is introduced by οὐ γάρ in 2:13 and concluded by the same device
in 3:22. The concluding οὐ γάρ of the second section
also functions as a transition and introduction to the
final section (3:22-4:25), the "power" of the gospel.

The concluding οὐ γάρ within the first two sections
probably performs a similar function. We may cite the
two references for purposes of comparison: οὐ γάρ ἐστιν
προσωπολημψία παρὰ τῷ θεῷ (For God shows no partiality,
2:11); οὐ γάρ ἐστιν διαστολή (For there is no distinction,
3:22). The import of both of these passages, whether with
respect to his wrath or with regard to his justification,
is that God shows no favoritism. What is determinative in
either case (i.e., wrath or justification) is one's response

to God's prior address, not what man himself is or is not capable of accomplishing. It is precisely from this basis that we may interpret the conclusion of the third section, the gospel as God's "power". The formal similarity between this conclusion and that of the preceding two sections is signalled by the introductory οὐκ in v. 23. We also have a functional similarity between this conclusion and that of the two preceding ones, but the conclusion in this instance functions simultaneously as the climax for the entire argument. The crucified and raised one is the demonstration of God's power and this aspect of the gospel, too, as in the conclusion of the preceding sections, is of divine origin. God's power, Jesus the Lord, is both the means of annulling wrath and of imparting justification to those who believe in him.

36. Unless the oath in 9:1 may be so interpreted.

37. John Knox (*The Interpreter's Bible,* 9 [Nashville: Abingdon Press, 1954], 578) suggests that these final sentences are not merely the conclusion of chs. 9-11 but of the entire argument from 1:16 forward. This suggestion fits well with my suggestion that the entire body-middle, i.e., 1:16-11:36, is executed as one continuous and artistic argument. Further proof that 11:36 is the conclusion of its section is the fact that the immediately succeeding verse (12:1) is a major transitional formula which introduces the paraenetic section of the letter.

38. οὐ γάρ: 7:15b, 19; 8:15; 9:6; 10:12; and 11:25f.; ἄρα οὖν: 5:18; 7:3; 21, 25; 8:1, 12; 9:16, 18; and 10:17; τί οὖν; 6:1, 15; 7:7, 13; 8:31; 9:14, 30; 11:1, 7, 11 (The last construction [τί οὖν] was analyzed in the applicative segment of the body-middle of Galatians [cf. comments on the fourth transition, 56 and n.34]. This rhetorical stereotyped question, as suggested previously [n.34], is characteristic of the *diatribe.*

There are other formulaic transitions in Part II of the body-middle which, though minor, have rather stereotyped forms. We may identify three such formulae in Rom. 5-11, the identifiable features of which may be set out as follows: (1) ὡς (or ὥσπερ)...οὕτως καί (5:12, 15, 18, 19, 21; 6:4, 10f., 19; 11:2, 5, 30. Cf. also Gal.1:9; 4:3; and 4:29; (2) οὐ μόνον...ἀλλὰ καί (1:32c; 4:12, 16, 23; 5:3, 11; 8:23; 9:10, 24); and (3) εἰ γάρ...πολλῷ μᾶλλον (5:10, 15, 17; 6:5; 11:12, 24). The first two formulae appear to perform a similar function, i.e., they are stereotyped means by which Paul introduces a new tack (or a new aspect) in the argument. These formulae serve a function similar to that of δὲ καί (cf. ch. I., 36f.), therefore, in the body-middle of the non-literary papyri, but they do not exercise the same major force in Paul. It is questionable, however, whether Paul is totally dependent on the epistolary tradition at this point. The first formula, for example, has at least partial parallels in the *diatribe* (cf. Bultmann, 42, 45. Cf. comments on the fifth transition also [οὕτως καί...] in the practical segment of the body-middle of Galatians [n.34].).

39. John Knox, "A Note on the Text of Romans," *NTS,* 2 (1955/6), 191-3 and "Romans 15:14-33 and Paul's Conception of His Apostolic Mission," *JBL,* 83(1964), 1-11. Both the general

character of the remarks in 1:8ff. as well as the treatise character of the body could well indicate that Rom. 1:1-15: 13 (if the references to Rome are omitted in 1:7, 15) was constructed by Paul as a general letter. The expression of the desire to visit in the body-opening disclosure formula, even if the formula was originally conceived in connection with the general letter, could hardly reflect an integral or specific relation to the body-middle, therefore, precisely because of the general nature of the body-middle. Unlike the common Greek letter or even other extant letters of Paul, therefore, the letter to the Romans is probably not prompted by a specific occasion.

40. Cf. 25 and n.37.

41. Funk, "The Apostolic *Parousia:* Form and Significance."

42. Funk notes (n. 1, 252) that this item does not seem to be regularly employed in the apostolic *parousia,* being peculiar to Rom. 15 (15b-21) and I Cor. 4 (15-16).

43. Item (5) may also be employed as a threat as both the subsequent analysis and Funk himself ("The Apostolic *Parousia,*" 264ff.) suggests.

44. Funk suggests (261) that benefit from the apostolic *parousia* accruing to the apostle (5a) or to apostle and congregation mutually (5a-b) indicates a friendlier letter than emphasis on benefit accruing to the recipients (5b): I Cor. 4; II Cor. 12:14ff.; Gal. 4.

45. The four formulae are: (1) the motivation for writing form (iii) of the disclosure formula (ch. I, 27); (2) responsibility statements (28-29); (3) the courtesy request for a letter (29); and (4) notification of a coming visit (29-31).

46. The reference to "speaking" (λέγω) in Gal. 5:2 is a recognizable substitute for the customary verb, γράφω.

47. The threat aspect emerges more clearly at each new stage within the body-closing. Thus, in the first unit of the body-closing of Philemon (the motivation for writing formula in v. 19), Paul states that Philemon should not hold anything against Onesimus and that he himself, if necessary, will repay any expenses which have been occasioned by Onesimus' absence. Paul also suggests, however, that it is actually Philemon who owes him. This latter suggestion, which could be construed as a veiled claim, is strengthened by Paul's command in v. 20 to "refresh his heart." This command is further strengthened in the second body-closing unit (the "confidence" phrase in v.21), where Paul states that he is confident that Philemon will do even *more* than he asks. And though the third body-closing unit (the intention to visit, the apostolic *parousia,* in v. 22) may imply an occasion of joy, it could prove threatening, if Philemon were uncooperative.

48. Paul states this explicitly in Phil. 1:6.

49. What amazes me most at this point, however, is the accuracy with which Funk was able to delineate the stages and function of the body-closing.

50. Only one discrete reference to Paul's purpose in writing is listed (II Cor. 13:10) and it is not one of the three speci-

fied here. It is not fortuitous, consequently, when he
states that item (1) does not loom so large in the Pauline
letters as it does in the non-literary papyri ("The Apostolic *Parousia*," n. 2, 260).

51. Cf. I. Cor. 5:3-5. One may also compare II Cor. 10:3-4 in
connection with the significance Paul attributed to his
presence.

52. Paul obviously felt that it was important, as the presence
of the three parallel references suggest (cf. first formula
on Table 1, p.61), to recapitulate the message of the letter. The reason for repeating the essence of the message,
at least on some occasions (probably both Philemon and
Galatians at this point), is integrally connected with Paul's
desire to spell out an appropriate response. This aspect
of the body-closing is also important in connection with
item (3) (the apostolic *parousia*). The response to this
initial claim circumscribes the basis from which either the
apostolic emissary or even Paul himself can proceed.

53. Cf. 29-31.

54. Taking a cue from John Knox at this point, he suggests that
Galatians was penned relatively late in Paul's career, at
a time when return to Galatia was impossible. The following
comments are especially appropriate: "In view of the magnitude of the crisis in Galatia, it is incredible that Paul
would not have backed up his letter with the hint of a future visit, had he been in a position to contemplate one,
however remote, or with the dispatch of an emissary, had
there been one available for the assignment. . . . This
can only mean that it was written at the time he had already
set his face to the west. Surely nothing less than that
would have prompted him to turn away with the mere wish
that he could be there now!" "The Apostolic *Parousia*,"
(266f.).

55. Both location, i.e., immediately following the second body-
closing unit, and formulaic features, e.g., the emphatic
form of the pronoun (ἐγώ) and the vocative, suggest such a
possibility.

56. We may better understand Gal. 6:17, perhaps, on this basis,
i.e., the "marks of Jesus" (again an explanation of Paul's
absence?) are proof of his apostleship.

57. One may consider this interpretation in relation to Paul's
statement in I Cor. 5:3-5: "For though absent in the body
I am present in spirit, and as if present, I have already
pronounced judgment in the name of the Lord Jesus on the
man who has done such a thing. When you are assembled, and
my spirit is present, with the power of our Lord Jesus,
you are to deliver this man to Satan for the destruction
of the flesh, that his spirit may be saved in the day of the
Lord Jesus." This latter passage certainly makes the interpretation of the former passage possible.
    Funk ("The Apostolic *Parousia*," 264f.) proposes the
use of II Cor. 10:3-4 in this connection: "For though we
live in the world we are not carrying on a worldly war,
for the weapons of our warfare are not worldly but have
divine power to destroy strongholds." If Paul thought of
his presence as the bearer of charismatic (eschatological?)
power, perhaps the impossibility of physical presence did
not prohibit the execution of his apostolic power.

58. Cf. the preceding review concerning work on the form of the Pauline letter (43-45). Cf. Funk, *Language, Hermeneutic, and Word of God,* 263-70, who sketches, in brief but careful scope, the principal contributions and contributors to the analysis of the form of the Pauline letter.

59. Exceptions to the form are: (1) Philemon is lacking the paraenetic section; (2) Galatians has no thanksgiving; and (3) Romans reverses the order of the body-closing and the paraenetical section, i.e., the apostolic *parousia* is usually immediately prior to the paraenesis but in Romans it comes immediately after. Funk suggests ("The Apostolic *Parousia,*" 267f.) a viable interpretation for the reverse order in Romans. He notes that Romans has two apostolic *parousia* sections, one of a more general nature (woven in-to the thanksgiving period, 1:8ff.) and one particularly related to the Roman congregation (15:14-33). He connects this idea with Knox's suggestion (cf. n.39) that Romans 1:1-15:13 was conceived by Paul as a circular letter. Paul needed to fill in only the address and perhaps, if necessary, a more personalized apostolic *parousia* at the end. Funk rightly notes that the customary form of the Pauline letter could scarcely have been so easily modified.

60. Schubert (16-27) suggests that I Thessalonians has no main body because the thanksgiving itself constitutes the body. In analogous manner, Robert Funk (*Language, Hermeneutic, and Word of God,* 273f.) assigns a special role to the apos-tolic *parousia* (the body-closing) in II Cor. 1-7. These letters, as well as Schubert's and Funk's interpreations, will be examined in more detail subsequently.

61. Both the possibility of innovation and evidence supporting inclusion of the usual elements will be taken up subse-quently at the appropriate points.

62. Schubert (16-27). He suggests that what at first glance looks like three separate thanksgivings, i.e., (1) 1:2-5, (2) 2:13f., and (3) 3:9-13, and two real digressions (i.e., the "first" thanksgiving turns into an intimate recital of the official and personal relationship between Paul and the Thessalonian church, 1:6-12; there is a similar "di-gression" between the "second" and "third" thanksgivings, namely, the discussion of Timothy's recent visit to Thes-salonica, 2:17-3:8) is only a stylistic device, employed elsewhere by Paul, to preserve the formal *unity* of the thanksgiving. From the point of view of form, function, and content, Schubert contends that the "digressions" are not digressions at all but are, on the contrary, fully legitimate and indeed constituitive elements of the general Pauline thanksgiving pattern. The progression of thought in the consistent repetition of the "antithesis" between writer and addressees, he notes, is a seamless robe unmis-takably characteristic of the thanksgiving from beginning to end, i.e., from 1:2-3:13. (The theme of the first di-gression is announced, for example, in 1:3f. and developed in vv. 6-10. Similarly, Paul's"apology," the second part of the first digression, is announced in 1:5b and developed in 2:1-12. In light of these observations, the "second" thanksgiving in 2:13f., therefore, is actually the stylistic climax to the entire digression, couched in the heightened language of the thanksgiving. Schubert suggests, in addi-

tion, that 2:17-3:13 is also a formal unit which in turn
is inseparable from the preceding part (1:2-2:16) of the
thanksgiving because it constitutes the final "eschatological" climax of the thanksgiving, an item characteristic of
the conclusion of the thanksgiving.).

Walter Schmithals ("Die Thessalonicherbriefe als Brief-
kompositionen," *Zeit und Geschichte*. Dankesgabe an Rudolf
Bultmann zum 80. Geburtstag, ed. E. Dinkler [Tübingen, 1964],
295-314) proposes, in connection with the multiple thanksgiving periods of I Thessalonians, a solution much different than that advocated by Schubert. He suggests that I
Thessalonians is a composite letter, with two prologues
(thanksgivings) and two conclusions. The two letters are:
(1) 1:1-2:12 + 4:3-5:28; (2) 2:13-4:2. The first of these
two letters, according to Schmithals, is complete in all
its parts. The second is not complete since it has neither
the opening preface nor the closing greetings. The redactor,
who put the two letters together, naturally excluded these
two elements in the second letter in order to produce the
composite letter.

Though I do not agree with Schmithals' interpretation of
the multiple thanksgivings (i.e., I agree with Schubert that
the nature of the epistolary situation was determinative
for the structural peculiarity; not, like Schmithals, that
each thanksgiving period indicates necessarily an additional
letter fragment), he is on the right track methodologically,
i.e., he attempts to understand the question of integrity
on "formal" grounds.

Schmithals proposes, in addition, that II Thessalonians
is also composite: a literary composition parallel to that of
I Thessalonians. The two letters are: (1) 1:1-12 + 3:6-16;
(2) 2:13, 14 + 2:1-12 + 2:15-3:5 + 17, 18 (The body precedes
the thanksgiving in this instance, according to Schmithals,
in order to avoid the juxtaposition of two prologues [thanks-
giving periods].). He contends that the redaction of both
I and II Thessalonians comes from the same hand, since they
give all the appearances of actual correspondence. One
could argue the latter point, of course, with entirely different premises, i.e., I Thessalonians (for reasons adduced
above) could be integral (and authentic) while II Thessalonians could have been penned by a later Paulinist who relied
on I Thessalonians as a structural Model. Cf. also T.W.
Manson, *Studies in the Gospels and Epistles* (Philadelphia:
Westminister, 1962), 259-275. Manson, following Johannes
Weiss (*Urchristentum*), suggested that both I and II Thess.
were Pauline, and that II Thess. was written first.

63. Schubert (26) rightly proposes, in my opinion, that the
thanksgiving contains all the primary information that
Paul wished to convey. No other subject within the letter
was equal in importance, from the author's point of view,
to the past anxiety and now the present rejoicing which
ensues from knowledge of the Thessalonians' faithfulness.

64. The eschatological climax which customarily concludes the
thanksgiving period is found at 1:10 in I Thessalonians,
immediately preceding the disclosure formula of 2:1. Apart
from this coincidence, which implies that the formula of
2:1 opens the body, it should be noted that no other major
formulaic construction, in the immediate context or at some
remove, could function in this capacity. The slightly ir-

regular form is due both to the past reference (i.e., rather than to the present) and to the Thessalonians' colloboration in the disclosure. See subsequent comments on 72.

65. External features cause I Thessalonians to appear dissimilar to the usual form of the body, but these external differences are due to the nature of the letter. Paul's message is customarily addressed to the present situation of the church to which he is writing, but the message of I Thessalonians concerns a past situation; a situation which colors all the elements of the body and which, concomitantly, is the basis for understanding the peculiar significance of the thanksgiving.

66. The background item does not always precede the disclosure formula (cf. ch. I, n. 16 and the background item, introduced subsequent to the disclosure formula, in Gal. 1:13f.) When the background item is introduced subsequent to the disclosure (or to a request), it is expressed by ἵνα, ὅπως, or γάρ clauses. The disclosure formula, when it is employed to open the body, does not ordinarily have a background item in the common Greek letter. Paul, on the other hand, seems to employ such an item regularly in the body-opening, whether he opens it with a request or the disclosure formula.

67. The entire section from 1:2-2:14ff. is characterized by the consistent repetition (recollection) of what "happened" (the Greek verb is γίνομαι) to Paul, the Thessalonians, and particularly the two mutually, when the gospel was preached at Thessalonica. Paul Schubert (19ff.) proposes in this connection that 1:5b, οἷοι ἐγενήθημεν ἐν ὑμῖν δι' ὑμᾶς ("You know what kind of men we proved to be among you for your sake."), is a topic sentence. Both this reference and eight remaining passages within the first two chapters of I Thessalonians contain the verb γίνομαι. All nine references are derived from and logically dependent on a remaining (the very first) reference in 1:5a: τὸ εὐαγγέλιον ἡμῶν ...ἐγενήθη εἰς ὑμᾶς...ἐν δυνάμει κτλ. ("our gospel came to you in power, etc."). Paul is the subject of the verb in five instances (1:5b; 2:1, 5, 7, 10), and we find the complementary form of the verb in the epistolary situation ἐγενήθητε (ὑμεῖς) four times (1:6, 7; 2:8,14). See additional comments and illustration on the use of this verb in I Thessalonians on 76f.

68. One group, taking advantage of Paul's being out of the way, was motivated by envy and strife and preached Christ in order to further their own designs. Another group was contributing to the apostle's sense of joy and triumph, however, because they preached Christ out of sincerity and a deep appreciation for Paul.

69. See n. 66.

70. Though both the Greek text and all of the English versions which I have examined place this verse with the succeeding paragraph, structurally it goes with the preceding verses.

71. The preceding proposal regarding the limits of the body sections, i.e., I Thess. 2:1-3:13; Phil. 1:12-2:30; I Cor. 1:10-4:21; II Cor. 1:8-7:16, was not intended to suggest that the material which succeeds each of these sections belongs necessarily to the paraenetical or letter-closing sections.

72. Robert W. Funk, *Language, Hermeneutic, and Word of God,* 272.

73. We should recognize that a diversity of opinion accrues to the nature of this section of I Thessalonians. Schmithals (cf. n.62), for example, proposes that the "thanksgiving" formula of v.13 is the beginning of an independent letter. Robert Funk (*Language, Hermeneutic and Word of God,* 265) calls 2:13-16 an "eschatological climax," suggesting thereby that the message segment of the body ("body-middle") has an eschatological conclusion. A number of 19th century interpreters, and more recently Birger Pearson, have argued that I Thess. 2:13-16 is a post-Pauline interpolation. We may consider Pearson's arguments ("I Thessalonians 2:13-16 as a Deutero-Pauline Interpolation," a paper read at the *AAR* Convention on Nov. 17, 1969 in Boston, Mass.) in connection with this latter interpretation. Pearson suggests that both the historical and the theological difficulties of this passage are so great that a post-Pauline interpolation theory must be entertained. He argues compellingly that the "wrath" which came upon the Jews in v.16 refers to a past event; an event which, in his opinion, could only have been the destruction of Jerusalem in A.D. 70. On this basis, the passage must have been penned post-70 A.D. Apart from such historical questions, he points out basic incompatabilities between this passage and Pauline theology. He notes, for example, that Paul does not attribute the death of Jesus to the Jews as this passage does; Paul never expresses the conception that God's wrath has come upon the Jewish people with utter finality; Paul could not have stated the "anti-Semitism" we find in v.15.

   Each of the above interpretations has merit, but I propose on formal grounds, not only that I Thess. 2:13-16 is Pauline (Schmithals, but *contra* Pearson) and that it plays an integral role within 2:13-3:13 (which is the body of only *one* letter according to Funk, and *contra* Schmithals) but also that it is the applicative (Part II) portion of the body-middle. Each of the preceding letters examined have included such a section, as an element within the letter and we should anticipate this section, therefore, in I Thessalonians. Both on formal grounds and on account of the interpretation previously adduced (71f.) regarding the repetition of the thanksgiving formula as an appropriate introduction to the applicative section of the body-middle of I Thessalonians, it is feasible to regard 2:13-16 as Part II of the body-middle. The real crux of the matter, perhaps, is not the thanksgiving in v.13 but the comparison between the Philippian Christians and the Jewish Christians of Judaea in vv. 14-16. On the surface at least, the language and ideas expressed in these verses do not appear Pauline. Taking Schubert's suggestion (77) that the thanksgiving announces the subject-matter of the letter as a point of departure, however, we may posit a formal link between what is announced in 1:6f. of the thanksgiving and 2:14ff. of the body. Note that the clause ὑμεῖς μιμηταί ...ἐγενήθητε of 1:6 is reflected in ὑμεῖς...μιμηταί ἐγενήθητε of 2:14 and the reference to tribulation in 1:6 may be picked up by the statement of suffering in 2:14.

74. This formulaic item (the perfect form of πείθω) is stated first in the thanksgiving (1:6); subsequently in the body-opening (1:14); the body-middle (1:25); and the body-closing (2:24).

75. The significance of the expression of "confidence" in Philippians raises an interesting question. Was the imprisonment in anyway determinative for Paul's adoption of the confidence phrase, as an item within the apostolic *parousia?* Or, does this imprisonment serve, rather, to validate a stance which Paul had already taken in relation to the gospel?

76. It was noted elsewhere (e.g., 47, 54ff. and n.34), however, that Part II tends to be less tightly constructed and the formulae usually vary from transition to transition.

77. Funk, *Language, Hermeneutic, and Word of God,* 264 f. He identifies an eschatological climax in the body of three letters (Phil. 2:14-18; I Thess. 2:13-16; I Cor. 4:1-13). He suggests that in each of these three letters the eschatological climax immediately precedes the apostolic *parousia* section. I agree with him in two instances (in Philippians and I Corinthians) that the exchatological climax is a discrete element within the body, but I have interpreted the remaining passage (I Thess. 2:13-16) differently (cf. n. 73 of this chapter).

    The eschatological conclusion in the body of Philippians and I Corinthians, unlike the climax of the thanksgiving, is geared specifically to the issue under discussion.

78. Translation: "For the word of the cross is (1) folly to those who are perishing, but (2) to us who are being saved it is the power of God."

79. "When I came to you, brethren, I did not come proclaiming to you the testimony of God in lofty words or wisdom (1). For I decided to know nothing among you except Jesus Christ and him crucified (2)."

80. "And I was with you...and my speech and my message were not in plausible words of wisdom, but in demonstration of the spirit and of power."

81. "But we impart a secret and hidden wisdom of God, (1) which God decreed before the ages...(2) None of the rulers of this age..."

82. "But I, brethren, could not address you as spiritual men,..."

83. "So let no one boast of men."

84. But see 2:2 which employs this construction and appears to be the reiteration of the opening theme: οὐ γὰρ ἔκρινά τι εἰδέναι ἐν ὑμῖν εἰ μὴ 'Ι. Χ. ...ἐσταυρωμένον. ("For I decided to know nothing among you except Jesus Christ ... crucified.")

85. Ulrich Wilckens, *Weisheit und Torheit: Eine exegetisch-religions geschichtliche Untersuchung zu I. Kor. 1 und 2 (Tübingen:* J. C. B. Mohr [Paul Siebeck], 1959). Wilcken's study is discussed by Robert Funk (*Language, Hermeneutic and Word of God,* 277-81).

86. "Word and Word in I Corinthians 2:6-16" (ch. 11 in *Language, Hermeneutic and Word of God,* 275-305), 283.

87. The two following transitions in 3:5 and 3:16 also exhibit formulaic features (interrogative τί with the conjunction οὖν in 3:5 and the perfect form of the disclosure formula in 3:16, but the transition in 3:18, introduced by the words

Μηδεὶς ἑαυτὸν ἐξαπατάτω, does not seem formulaic (but see Wilckens, 8, on the significance of this formula). The transition in 3:18, however, summarizes the lineaments of the argument from 3:1-17. The following transition in 3:21 should probably be taken as the resolution of the argument. Note that these latter two points of transition employ the imperative (the applicative segment of the body-middle of Philippians, the transitions in 1:27 and 2:1, was also characterized by the use of the imperative).

88. "I wanted to come to you first, so that you might have... pleasure;..."

89. Günther Bornkamm, *Die Vorgeschichte des Sogenannten Zweiten Korintherbriefes,* Sitzungsberichte der Heidelberger Akademie der Wissenschaften, Philosophischhistorische Klasse, Jahrgang 1961, 2. Abhandlung (Heidelberg: Carl Winter, 1961); English summary in *NTS* 8 (1962), 258-64.

90. Robert Funk, *Language, Hermeneutic, and Word of God,* 273f.

91. "Travelogue" is the older designation for what Funk calls subsequently "Apostolic *Parousia.*"

92. *Lanaguage, Hermeneutic, and Word of God,* 273f.

93. Funk (*Language, Hermeneutic, and Word of God,* 263, n.52) calls attention to the closely articulated nature of this section. He points to the use of ἐχώ (with οὗτος, τοιοῦτος, αὐτός) at 3:4, 12; 4:1, 7, 13 to renew the basic theme in a new way. We should note that this theme of "having" (ἐχώ) and "not-having" is also characteristic of the body-closing sections (cf. 1:15; 2:3, 4; and 7:5). Similarly, the theme of confidence which we identified as a characteristic of the body-closing sections (see the various references to "being confident," πεποιθώς, and "confidence," πεποίθησις, in the outline on 81f.: 1:15a; 2:3b; 3:4; 7:4) is threaded through the defense of Paul's apostolic office in 2:14-7:4.

94. Schubert, 71-77 (especially 76f.). We could suggest, on Schubert's analysis, that this first unit in the body-closing, analogous to I Thessalonians, does not mention the act of writing because only Paul's presence can convey his joy. Subsequent analysis will show, however, that another reason lies behind Paul's failure to call attention to the letter itself.

95. The specific problem at Philippi, concerning some kind of disharmony, is intimated in the immediately succeeding section (1:27ff). Paul commands the Philippians (1:30), consequently, to imitate his own manner of life. The hymn of 2:6-11 is also employed to summon the Philippians to the imitation of the crucified Christ.

96. Cf. 2:25. He had been ill some months prior and was presumably well at this point, since enough time had elapsed for message of his illness to pass to Philippi and back. Homesickness was no excuse for leaving his post.

97. Epaphroditus probably carried the letter to ensure him a good reception. This explanation accounts for the description of his qualifications. The Philippians were to know he came as Paul's emissary and, therefore, they were to take him fully into their counsels.

98. The purpose for writing is not signalled by a discrete construction, but we found a similar state of affairs elsewhere (e.g., the purpose was variously introduced by ἴνα, ὅτι, ὡς in Philemon, Galatians, and Romans).

99. This second item of the first body-closing unit is abbreviated, for purpose of diagram, in Table 2.

100. Robert Funk, "The Apostolic *Parousia*: Form and Significance," 249-68. The reader may also refer to the presentation of Funk's analysis of items in this study (60ff.) in relation to the tabulation of items for each passage, in the order of their occurrence, in Table 2.

1. The six body-opening formulae are: (1) the fuller form (i) of the disclosure formulae (Gal. 1:11; Rom. 1:13; I Thess. 2:1; Phil. 1:12; II Cor. 1:8); (2) the request formula (Philem. 8ff.; I Cor. 1:10); (3) joy expressions (Philem 7; Phil. 4:10); (4) the expression of astonishment (Gal. 1:6); (5) the statement of compliance (Gal. 1:9); (6) the formulaic use of ἀκούω (Gal. 1:13f.).

2. Five of the twelve body-opening formula examined (cf. the 12 listed in n. 1 above) were the fuller form of the disclosure formula. The remaining seven references were distributed among five types of formulae.

3. This form is found in two of the five occurrences of the body-opening disclosure formula (Rom. 1:13 and II Cor. 1:8). The form of the formula in the remaining three references is: γνωρίζι γὰρ ὑμῖν, ἀδελφοί, ...ὅτι in Gal. 1:11; γινώσκειν δὲ ὑμᾶς βούλομαι, ἀδελφοί, ὅτι... in Phil. 1:12; and Αὐτοὶ γὰρ οἴδατε, ἀδελφοί,..ὅτι in I Thess. 2:1). This form of the disclosure formula is also found in I Cor. 10:1; 12:1; and Rom. 11:25.

4. Whereas the joy expression is tied to the arrival of a letter in the non-literary papyri, and may function as the background to a request for further correspondence, the joy expression in Philem. 7 functions as the background from which Paul makes a material request. And, whereas the verb of hearing is tied to an expression of grief or anxiety in the papyri, the report conveyed by the verb in Gal. 1:13 is not connected with either an expression of grief or anxiety. Similarly, Paul takes liberties in his use of the body-opening disclosure formulae. The disclosure formula in the body-opening of the non-literary papyri, for example, is usually a self-contained unit, but Paul employs background items in connection with the disclosure formulae, e.g., the use of 3 additional body-opening formulae in Galatians as background items for the disclosure formula (cf. 49ff.).

5. These four body-closing formulae are: (1) the motivation for writing form (iii) of the disclosure formula (cf. analysis, ch. I, 27); (2) responsibility statements (28-29); (3) the courtesy request for a letter (29); and (4) notification of a coming visit (29-31).

6. I say "surrogate" because, though the formula does employ the verb meaning "to write," γράφω, as in the papyri, Paul does not actually state the convention as a disclosure (i.e., he does not use the verb "to know," γινώσκω). In addition, the function of the summons to responsibility (the "responsibility statement") is not conveyed by a separate construction but is implicit in Paul's motivation for writing statement, i.e., the construction becomes a hybrid motivation for writing-*responsibility* formula in Paul.

BIBLIOGRAPHY

Books

Bjerkelund, Carl J. *Parakalô: Form, Funktion und Sinn der para-kalô-Satze in den paulinischen Briefen.* ("Bibliotheca Theologica Norvegica," 1) Oslo: Universitetsforlaget, 1967.

Blass, F. and Debrunner, A. *A Greek Grammar of the New Testament and Other Early Christian Literature.* Translated and revised by Robert W. Funk. Chicago: University of Chicago Press, 1961.

Bornkamm, Günther. *Die Vorgeschichte des sogenannten Zweiten Korintherbriefes.* Sitzungsberichte der Heidelberger Akademie der Wissenschaften. ("Philosophischhistorische Klasse," Jahrgang 1961, 2. Abhandlung) Heidelberg: Carl Winter, 1961.

Bultmann, Rudolf. *Exegetische Probleme des zweiten Korintherbriefes.* ("Symbolae Biblicae Upsalienses," Supplementhäfaten til Svensk Exegetisk Arsbok 9) Uppsala, 1947.

_____. *Der Stil der paulinischen Predigt und die kynisch-stoische Diatribe.* "Forschungen zur Religion und Literature des Alten und Neuen Testaments," No. 13. Göttingen: Vandenhoeck & Ruprecht, 1910.

Deissman, Adolf. *Bible Studies.* Translated by A. Grieve. Edinburgh: T & T Clark, 1901.

Dibelius, Martin. *Der Brief des Jacobus* (11th ed.). Enlarged by Heinrich Greeven. "Meyers Kommentar," vol. 15. Göttingen: Vandenhoeck & Ruprecht, 1964.

Exler, F. J. *The Form of the Ancient Greek Letter: A Study in Greek Epistolography.* Ph.D. dissertation, Catholic University of America, 1923.

Funk, Robert W. *Language, Hermeneutic, and Word of God.* New York: Harper & Row, 1966.

Horn, R. C. *The Use of the Subjunctive and Optative Moods in the Non-Literary Papyri.* Ph.D. dissertation, Philadelphia, 1926.

Knox, John. *Philemon Among the Letters of Paul.* Nashville and New York: Abingdon Press, 1959.

Koskenniemi, Heikki. *Studien zur Idee und Phraseologie des griechischen Briefes bis 400 n. Chr.* Annales Academiae Scientiarum Fennicae. ("Sarja-Ser. B. Nide-Tom.," 102, 2) Helsinki, 1956.

Mayser, Edwin M. *Grammatik der griechischen Papyri aus der Ptolemäerzeit.* 2 vols. Berlin-Leipzig, 1906-38.

Preisigke, Friedrich, and Kiessling, Emil. *Wörterbuch der griechischen Papyruskunden.* 3 vols. Berlin: selbstverlag der Erben, 1925-29.

Rigaux, Béda. *Letters of Saint Paul. Contemporary Studies.* Translated by Carrol and Ynoick. New York: Herder & Herder, 1968.

129

Roller, Otto. *Das Formular der paulinischen Briefe: Ein Beitrag zur Lehre vom antiken Briefe*. Stuttgart: W. Kohlhammer, 1933.

Schubert, Paul. *Form and Function of the Pauline Thanksgivings*. Beihefte zur *Zeitschrift für die neutestamentliche Wissenschaft*, 20. Berlin: Töpelmann, 1939.

Thyen, Hartwig. *Der Stil der jüdisch-hellenistischen Homilie*. "Forschungen zur Religion und Literatur des Alten und Neuen Testaments," No. 47. Göttingen: Vandenhoeck & Ruprecht, 1955.

Turner, Eric Gardener. *Greek Papyri: An Introduction*. Princeton University Press, 1968.

White, John L. *The Form and Structure of the Official Petition*. SBL Dissertation Series 5. Missoula, Montana: Scholars' Press, 1972.

Wilckens, Ulrich. *Weisheit und Torheit: Eine exegetisch-religions geschichtliche Untersuchung zu 1. Kor. 1 und 2*. Tübingen: J. C. B. Mohr [Paul Siebeck], 1959.

Winter, John. *Life and Letters in the Papyri*. Ann Arbor: University of Michigan Press, 1933.

Ziemann, F. *De Epistularum Graecarum Formulis Sollemnibus Quaestiones Selectae*. Berlin: Haas, 1912.

Articles, Essays, and Unpublished Material

Funk, Robert W. "The Apostolic *Parousia*: Form and Significance." In *Christian History and Interpretation: Studies Presented to John Knox*, pp. 249-268. Edited by W. R. Farmer, C. F. D. Moule, and R. R. Niebuhr. Cambridge: Cambridge University Press, 1967.

Knox, John. "A Note on the Text of Romans." *New Testament Studies*, II (1955/56), 191-93.

_____. "Romans 15:14-33 and Paul's Conception of His Apostolic Mission." *Journal of Biblical Literature*, LXXXIII (1964), 1-11.

Mullins, Terence Y. "Greeting as a New Testament Form." *Journal of Biblical Literature*, LXXXVII (December, 1968), 418-26.

_____. "Petition as a Literary Form," *Novum Testamentum*, V (January, 1962), 46-54.

Pearson, Birger. "I Thessalonians 2:13-16 as a Deutero-Pauline Interpolation." A paper read at the annual meeting of the American Academy of Religion (November 17, 1969).

Robinson, James. "Die Hodajot-Formel in Gebet und Hymnus des Frühchristentums." *Apophoreta. Festschrift für Ernst Haenchen*, pp. 194-235. Edited by W. Eltester. Berlin: Töpelmann, 1964.

Sanders, Jack T. "The Transition from Opening Epistolary Thanksgiving to Body in the Letters of the Pauline Corpus." *Journal of Biblical Literature*, LXXXI (December, 1962), 348-62.

Schmithals, Walter. "Die Thessalonicherbriefe als Briefkompo-
sitionen." *Zeit und Geschichte. Dankesgabe an Rudolf Bultmann zum 80. Geburtstag,* pp. 295-314. Edited
by E. Dinkler. Tübingen, 1964.

Wendland, Paul. "Die urchristlichen Literaturformen." *Handbuch
zum Neuen Testament* I, 3, pp. 339-45. Tübingen: J. C.
B. Mohr [Paul Siebeck], 1912.